There are five good reasons why you should read this book. First, it is very well written and produced. The style is informal yet precise, articulate without being too academic. I can see MBA students and managing directors getting pleasure from reading this book. Second, it really is imaginative and different, looking at familiar issues from a very different perspective. Third, the author is very unusual in that he is well informed about two often very disparate areas (i.e. real business and music), which he links together brilliantly. Few people have the depth of knowledge or insight into these worlds as much as Peter Cook. Fourth, what he covers is important. He brings a very fresh approach to some fundamentally important issues in business. Rarely are business books such a good read. Fifth, you can treat the book as a tapas meal, as dim sum or a full feast. Some may enjoy dipping in, others enjoy the whole book at a 'full sitting'.

Professor Adrian Furnham, University College London

Original, perceptive, effective and amusing... Peter Cook's unique take on the parallel universes of Business and Rock music never fails to stimulate, inspire and entertain. There are more ideas in here than in a dozen self-help manuals... and even if you DON'T get to Number One, you'll have a damned good laugh trying.

Richard Strange, Founder of the Doctors of Madness

Peter provides some very thought provoking moments on management and leadership using some unexpected musical metaphors and lessons. Amongst my highlights, I love that "The

Darkness are Queen without disco" and that this relates to the fact that "Companies can learn parallel lessons by adopting a mindset that looks to the future whilst respecting cultural signifiers of the past". Clever and conscience pricking stuff. Well done.

Stephen Bourne, Commercial Manager, Janssen-Cilag Ltd,
A Johnson and Johnson Company

A book of management lessons drawn from the world of music. Original and great fun to read. Peter Cook lubricates 'dry' management theory in the most original way. This book is not 'just another book on business', it is original and fun to read due to the author's unique ability to teach and illustrate management theory through combining academic thinking with case studies from the world of music.

Tina Bauer, Manager, HP Enterprise Services

A highly enjoyable read that eases you through the four themes of the book: Strategy, Creativity, Innovation and Leadership. Quite the opposite of a dull textbook.

Jon Beaman, Senior Director, Pfizer

A business management book that is stimulating and without complication. In this book, Peter Cook weaves his experiences from the music industry and business management into a useful and entertaining guide to business practices. Simple yet fundamentally sound!

Richard McCullough, The United Nations

This book is for my wife Alison and my children, Thomas and James. With love and thanks for Alison's tireless help, support and tolerance at the constant barrage of projects and questions that I throw at her. For Tom and Jim, in the hope that their curiosity and thirst for learning will serve them throughout their life.

The Music of Business

**Business excellence
fused with music**

Peter Cook

SECOND EDITION

The Academy of Rock

Cultured Llama Publishing
11 London Road
Teynham, Sittingbourne
ME9 9QW
www.culturedllama.co.uk

ISBN 978-0-9932119-1-1

Printed in Great Britain by Lightning Source UK Ltd

Managing Editor and typographical design: Bob Carling

Jacket design: Peter Birkett, Das Ist Design, info@peterbirkettsculptor.co.uk
www.peterbirkettsculptor.co.uk

Contents

www.academy-of-rock.co.uk   **Peter Cook**

Peter Cook   www.academy-of-rock.co.uk

Introduction

For 20 years now, I have written, spoken and consulted on the parallels between the business universe and the world of music, be it rock, jazz, classical etc. This follows my much longer involvement with three passions: Science, Business and Music. Having taught leaders around the world, I've been astonished and delighted to find that many others see the parallels as well. Science and the arts are "separated at birth" through our education system, yet it's clear that some of the greatest science has been conceived through the arts and vice versa. My great passion is to break down these artificial divisions as these are where the sweet spots of great thinking and doing occur.

In 'The Music of Business' I bring together a set of bite-sized articles to provoke and inspire you to think and act differently about a number of business topics, in ways that are better than the usual fare. In short, this book offers you a rapid digest of business wisdom without all the business jargon.

We mainly work with these ideas live, in conferences and keynotes, working with professional musicians and music celebrities as and when required. If you like this book, share it with colleagues, customers, clients and contacts to start the positive revolution for business ideas that reach your mind, body and soul.

Peter Cook   www.academy-of-rock.co.uk

Contact me at peter@humdyn.co.uk, via the websites www. academy-of-rock.co.uk and www.humdyn.co.uk, phone ++44 (0) 7725 927585, SKYPE petercook2020

PART 1 – Strategy

Introduction to Part I – Strategy

In this part of the book we examine business strategy from a number of diverse perspectives. In a turbulent world, strategy is a continuous process of reconnaissance, involving colleagues, clients, customers and competitors. Execution of strategy requires responsiveness and the ability to change course mid-stream, whilst not flitting from fad to fad.

We start with the safe haven of 'sticking to the knitting' with the example of AC/DC, a rock band that have stayed close to home with their music for over 40 years, like Status Quo and The Rolling Stones. Sticking to your strategy is only good if your markets are stable and customers seek consistency. A creative exaggeration of the U2 song "I Still Haven't Found What I'm Looking For" opens up the strategy debate further, as we explore emergent strategy via the medium of Frederick Herzberg, Bono and De Bono. This is a theme we return to later in the book when we examine the leadership of learning companies.

Steve Mostyn offers us a window on Led Zeppelin's business excellence model via a look at Peter Grant's uncompromising leadership of the band, which put the musician's interests before that of the vampiric music industry.

Sometimes it's just as easy to learn from mistakes as it is successes, especially if those mistakes are not your own. We take a lighthearted view at the spoof movie 'This is Spinal Tap' and my own experience in trying to launch the real Spinal Tap tour for lessons from strategic failure. At the same time we look at parallel lessons from my own experience in sponsoring a round the world rock tour that was a glorious failure.

After a brief night at the opera, we have a look at the question of magic bullets in business. Suffice to say that there are no magic strategic bullets in a rapidly changing business world, although we develop some principles on which to formulate your approach to an agile business. We also take a look inside the music business with a view to learning about reinvention via the piece 'Living in the Past'. It becomes clear that repeat performances are the order of the day in many cases and this is often mirrored in business practice. It takes great courage to break away from accepted paradigms in music and in business although we are in an age where 'business as unusual' is the norm. We look at some examples of this later in the book.

Professor Tim Kastelle brings us right up to date with an interesting experiment in new business models via his example of The Kaiser Chiefs, which again turns received wisdom on it's head. Will their attempt to use mass personalisation and crowdsourcing as a means of reaching, engaging and retaining their fans work? Time will tell. In a related piece we look at two examples of crowdfunding as a strategy for engaging people with your venture or enterprise. Enterprise inside your company is a theme we return to via a piece first written for Sir Richard Branson's Virgin brand.

Finally we take some lessons on economics, not from John Maynard Keynes or Adam Smith, but via the medium of heavyweight rockers Genesis and Led Zeppelin, from the desk of Andrew Sentance, Senior Economic Adviser, PwC

(PricewaterhouseCoopers) and former Monetary Policy Adviser at The Bank of England. Andrew is also a collaborator in a rock band called Rock In The City that aims to humanise the square mile through music.

"Life is what happens when you're busy making other plans"

John Lennon

Sticking to the knitting: AC/DC

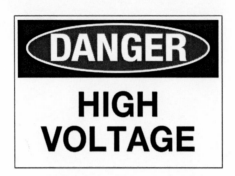

Have you ever been to an AC/DC concert? What can we learn from AC/DC about business and high voltage performance? Check out "You Shook Me All Night Long" on YouTube to get a crash course in DC. AC/DC start a concert as if they are already on the encore. What would happen if you started your business meetings as if they were all over before they started? With difficult decisions taken, staff energised, excited and engaged about their part in the business? It's a different approach to the anticlimax method to business meetings. What else can we learn from AC/DC about business strategy, culture and branding?

Before I get into trouble here, let me say that I love AC/DC's work, having first seen them in 1975 in a sweaty Council hall in South East England. I was just inches away from Angus Young and Bon Scott. Life was never the same... But, in my opinion as a musician, AC/DC's success lies in the fact that they have not really innovated to a great degree. More or less the same few chords arranged in a different order over 35 years have kept people coming back for more of the same. Slightly harsh you may say? Well, what I mean by this is that AC/DC have not switched genres – they have not done 'Country and Western', hip-hop, rap or dealt with 'space themes' such as David Bowie. This has given them immense sales to people who like consistency and reliability over artists such as Prince et al, whose motto is 'expect the unexpected'.

The quality that business thought leader Tom Peters calls 'sticking to the knitting' has served them very well indeed. AC/DC's album "Back in Black" was the 2nd highest selling album in history, after "Thriller" by Michael Jackson. So, what has this to do with business strategy?

In business, conventional wisdom says that it pays to have a strong culture/brand, such as Ryanair and Ikea. Indeed Ryanair has such a strong culture that I've discovered people who have a love/hate relationship with the brand even if they have not travelled on one of their aircraft! This is one of the acid tests of a strong culture/brand – you know what the brand/product/ service is all about before you have ever experienced it.

Moreover, there is no difference in the external perception of the brand and the internal culture that supports it. Even if you hate Ryanair, it's impossible to deny that they clearly state what you will be getting 'on the tin' – low cost travel, with nothing else added, take it or leave it. Ryanair is a textbook example of alignment of strategy with what takes place on the ground, even though Michael O'Leary detests management consultants, MBAs and management thinking, having once written to me on the topic. See his strident reply to my letter:

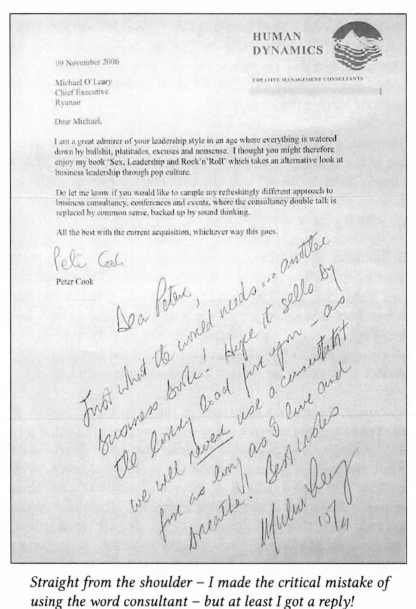

Straight from the shoulder – I made the critical mistake of using the word consultant – but at least I got a reply!

Peter Cook   www.academy-of-rock.co.uk

A strong culture arises when all the 'hard and soft' elements of what makes up a culture come together in a seamless whole. Johnson's model of the so-called 'paradigm' is instructive here – see below for the paradigm model. If all these elements are aligned and linked, you have a strong culture. Ryanair is a very strong culture as typified by the fact that customers who have not travelled on the airline already know what to expect.

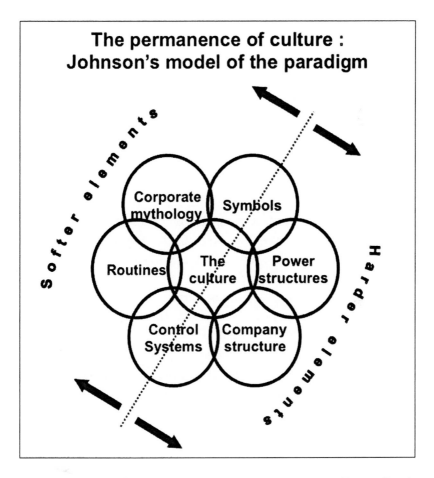

**The permanence of culture :
Johnson's model of the paradigm**

Softer elements

Harder elements

Corporate mythology

Symbols

Routines

The culture

Power structures

Control Systems

Company structure

However, when market change, strong cultures can fail to adapt. For example Sony did not respond to music downloading and the digital music revolution because they had a record company. This assisted Sony in their decline from market domination to a company playing catch up over many years. Marks and Spencer lost hold of the market and did a number of high-handed things such as refusing to take credit cards, which lost them business in an "I Want It All, I Want It Now" consumer society.

Marks and Spencer also attempted to expand into Europe using an ethno-centric (that's British in English!) approach to business, in the mistaken belief that their brand was bigger than the customer, with disastrous consequences. I am left wondering just what Ryanair would do if they faced fundamental challenges to their low cost strategy over an extended period.

So a strong culture with an unchanging brand and business offering CAN be a route to long-term commercial success, but you need a stable market for this. AC/DC, Status Quo, and The Rolling Stones know all about stability. However, in turbulent times, rock stars and companies ALSO need to learn how to adapt and become a true learning company if they are to survive and thrive. This is rather different than being blown about by the wind or latest business fad.

We look at Prince later on in this book, as someone who has adapted and largely kept his audience base, even though he has tested their patience to destruction. We also look at Britney Spears in a whimsical way, through the title of her mega hit

"Oops I Did It Again" as an instructive insight into becoming a Learning Company.

Companies such as Toyota, Virgin, Apple and Unilever, have been successful at maintaining a strong culture whilst adapting their offer to meet new customer needs. At one point, Toyota promised the biggest range of car models ever seen in a mass production market. We explore Steve Jobs' and Apple's approach to innovation later on in this book. In Unilever's case, they have been particularly adept at reaching into their audiences to engage them in discovering unfulfilled needs. Unilever

"Whole Lotta Business"
Rowena Sian Morgan
with her AC / DC
Gibson SG

Peter Cook

have also been pioneers in the use of crowdsourcing to engage their customers in the process of staying ahead and adapting to change.

You will find our interview with Chris Slade, AC/DC's drummer at our YouTube channel and on the website www.academy-of-rock.co.uk/music-biz

AC/DC strategy lesson # 1. The smart money is on being a creature of habit, whilst also remaining nimble and flexible to respond to your audience, customers or marketplace.

AC/DC strategy lesson # 2. Resist the temptation to change every week, according to this week's fad or fashion. That way can lead to becoming a one-hit wonder. A learning company need not be schizophrenic in its attempts to change.

AC/DC strategy lesson # 3. Whatever you decide to change, ensure your customers see a connection to your core brand so that they can follow with confidence.

"It's a long way to the top if you
wanna Rock'n'Roll"

AC/DC

I Still Haven't Found What I'm Looking For: U2 on strategy

U2's song "I Still Haven't Found What I'm Looking For" is obviously not about business strategy. Rather a long-term search for a part-time lover by the Irish crooner Bono, or possibly a call to more creativity from the business guru Edward de Bono! Nonetheless this does not stop me pointing out what Henry Mintzberg observed, that business strategy is often an 'emergent' function of business, where strategic plans are seen as flexible templates to guide a general line of action, but not recipes to be followed ad nauseam.

Here are five other critical strategic issues that the modern business strategist should be aware of. Unfortunately U2 have not covered these points in their songs!

I Still Haven't Found What I'm Looking For:
The importance of emergent strategy

Deliberate strategy

Realised strategy

Intended strategy

Unintended strategy

Emergent strategy

Peter Cook   www.academy-of-rock.co.uk

1. Strategic planning is no longer a head office function in most companies. Strategy is distributed and is the responsibility of everyone. That does not mean to say that chaos should reign. To achieve a sense of alignment in a complex adaptive system requires excellent communications, top-down, bottom-up and laterally. This is especially true of companies who are exposed to their customers via the internet where strategy may be partly informed by customer perception/desire. To read more on science of complexity and chaos, refer to James Gleick's work in this area and Professor Charles Handy's book "The Age of Unreason" for a lighter viewpoint.

2. Sustainable competitive advantage arises from differences between firms, not similarities. Thus, if you are in close proximity to a competitor in terms of products, services, geography and so on, one strategic option is to create a difference that creates space between you. This may of course mean that you compete better. It may simply open up the market in ways that means everyone can gain a share.

3. Foresight is better than hindsight. In order to know before the competition is going to head you off at the pass, we need dynamic approaches to strategy, rather than static use of models, which tell you 'what happened', rather like driving a car using the rear view mirror. Approaches such as 'Scenario Modelling', 'War Gaming' and 'Projective Methodologies' to help companies pre-empt decisions by competitors and in a number of other ways to seize advantage. To read more on the art of war for executives, read Donald Krause's work on Sun Tzu's seminal thinking in this area.

4. In some cases strategy is all about leveraging a firm's tacit knowledge and processes, which may not be easily copied or appropriated. Put simply, taking advantage of your collective brainpower rather than the physical assets you own. Exemplars of this approach to strategy would include Apple and Facebook. In particular Apple have a culture that enables it to limit leakage of its proprietary knowledge, even though its people leave the offices at the end of every day. However, designing and implementing a strategy to harness brainpower is simpler to write down than it is to put into practice.

5. Companies need to be continuously sensing weak signals of change in the business environment, so that your company may head the competition off by staying one step ahead. These days such 'weak signals' of impending change may come from staff who are in the customer's environment or even from the customers themselves through approaches such as 'crowdsourcing'.

So, Bono's lyric, "I Still Haven't Found What I'm Looking For", reframed using de Bono's lateral thinking approach in the context of business strategy, may not be such a bad thing. If strategy is a continuous and constant process of readjustment, the hunger to learn rapidly and respond to ever changing market needs is a core competence. Who would have thought it possible to gain so much business wisdom from just eight words of a pop song?

Peter Cook   www.academy-of-rock.co.uk

"And she's buying a stairway to heaven"

Led Zeppelin on Strategy

Whole Lotta Love: Business lessons from Led Zeppelin

Chris Welch's obituary of Peter Grant in The Independent newspaper stated his achievements well.

> *"It was Grant who arranged their deal with Atlantic Records in 1968, then hailed as one of the biggest in industry history. He never interfered with their music, but was a 'hands-on' manager who travelled the world with his charges to ensure their financial and physical well-being. Led Zeppelin became extremely wealthy from the sales of millions of albums and concert tickets during their 12-year reign from 1968 to 1980".*

Behind the myth of Led Zeppelin and Peter Grant is evidence of management thinking and action that gives the 21st century manager some new insights.

In 1966 Jimmy Page joined The Yardbirds. With his childhood friend Jeff Beck, touring sold out venues across America. Touring success but financial failure left the band wondering how to even meet food bills. Poor management was to blame. Beck left the group leaving Page to assume control of the frustrated outfit. The band's management duties were passed on to Grant and by 1968 the pre-cursor to Led Zeppelin, The New Yardbirds were formed.

Grant's management transformed the band. So what did Grant do that we can learn from?

Grow and support talent

The first role of a manager of creative people is to grow and develop talent, nurturing and most importantly getting out of the way of the creative process. Grant's obsessive support for the band was outstanding, from ensuring the member's financial well being to ensuring that they were always ready to wow their audience on a demanding 45 shows as part of a 50-day tour. He also created a close team of publicity, security, sound engineers, roadies and financial managers that were the core support team to the band's success. Grant deliberately refocused attention on the needs of the artists, often at the expense of the record companies, tour promoters and other agents.

Challenge accepted business processes

Grant's paradoxical PR and publicity strategy created a genuine grass roots mass underground following. His refusal for TV appearances of the band and refusal to release singles were key to Led Zeppelin's word of mouth rise and ongoing media mystique. Coupled with this was his radical re-negotiating of promoters' fees from 90% to 10% of door revenue. Grant quoted by Welch.

> "The days of the promoter giving a few quid to the group against the money take on the door are gone. Managers, agents, and promoters ran the business when the funny thing is it's the groups who bring the people in. I thought the musicians would be the people who get the wages".

Editor's note: The 90:10 approach is still alive and well as I write this book, with many young bands assuming that they must pay to play and that exploitation of artists is a normal part of the music business.

Grant's approach to marketing would not be out of place in the 21st century where crowdsourcing and customer experience and engagement are the watchwords of business. Today it is recognised that profits come from well managed live performances as opposed to music sales. Grant laid the foundation stones that Beyoncé to U2 have benefited from. Promoters' assumptions about margin had well and truly been challenged. The creation of Swan Song record label in the 1970s was a further act of controlling market access.

Inspire a shared vision

Grant's insistence that Led Zeppelin could (and would) be the world's greatest Rock'n'Roll act was the push and belief that allowed Page, Plant, Bonham and Jones to do their best.

The leverage behind the Atlantic Records deal in 1968 was evidence of that. Atlantic Records granted them a $200,000 advance before Atlantic president Ahmet Ertegun had even seen the band.

Let leaders lead

The paradox of management is the confusion of leadership and management. Both are key to organisation success. In a Rock'n'Roll band the band leader is almost never the manager.

Peter Cook   www.academy-of-rock.co.uk

Grant allowed distributed leadership to develop within the band, from founder Jimmy Page, 'front man' Robert Plant, with the world's leading drummer John Bonham to intellectual philosopher and bass leader John Paul Jones.

Create and enforce governance

Governance is the often-overlooked duller part of the manager's toolkit. Once Grant established copyright, he was renowned for his frequent personal enforcement of fake merchandisers and bootleggers. Welch comments:

> *"People were terrified of him. He rode roughshod over anyone who tried to get in his way and he wasn't scared of anyone, police, promoters or officials".*

In the 1970s Led Zeppelin was the most profitable band in rock history. Grant's attention to detail was also noted, from his assessment of the quality of PA equipment to lighting sequences to the attention to the fine detail of his accountant's profit and loss accounts and tax status advice.

Summary

Led Zeppelin's management by Peter Grant is a classic tale:

1. Talent management and good HR practice.
2. Competitive strategy by daring to be different.
3. Using visionary approaches to leadership to create.
4. Allowing for distributed leadership within the enterprise.
5. Ensuring that intellectual property is valued and guarded.

www.academy-of-rock.co.uk   Peter Cook

This article was written by Steve Mostyn, Associate Fellow, Saïd Business School, Executive Education. Steve may be reached at www.steve-mostyn.com

"Improvisation is too good to leave to chance"

Paul Simon

Spinal Tap and strategic mis-management

You could attend a three-week executive master class to learn the principles of project management or take a Prince 2 project management certification programme. However, to learn about the practical stuff could take you a lifetime and involve learning from expensive mistakes as well as successes. So, is there a way to learn about strategic execution and project management quickly and without risk by examining the spoof rockumentary "This Is Spinal Tap"? Of course there is! Check out the classic "Stonehenge" sequence on YouTube with a cup of coffee or a Jack Daniels whilst reading this chapter.

The Spinal Tap Stonehenge sequence is a sorry tale of poor project management... the gap between expectations and the outcome. Just before the sequence starts, a drawing of Stonehenge is drawn on a napkin by the group's guitarist and handed to the scenery designer by the band's manager. This is unwittingly taken as a definitive project specification for the manufacture of the piece of scenery.

Unfortunately all the project resources are committed to the 'model' based on the dimensions (in inches rather than feet). This casual mistake by the guitarist Nigel Tuffnel results in the production of an exact replica of Stonehenge, but with a 12 fold reduction in the dimensions of 18 inches × 3 inches!

Of course, in "This Is Spinal Tap", the band is then forced to execute their strategy using the microscopic Stonehenge model due to lack of budget to correct the mistake. They attempt to accommodate the dramatic understatement in size by using dwarfs to work alongside the model and bringing the Stonehenge model down from the heavens onto the stage to give it greater 'height' and 'gravitas', but it is clear that they have failed. When plotted against traditional project management approaches, it is obvious that the problem lies at the start of the process:

You may rightly say, "Well, this is a Hollywood comedy movie and nothing like real life". Not at all. Indeed, the reason why "This Is Spinal Tap" is so awfully funny is because the sequences are all based on real life events that have occurred in the rock business and the business world in general.

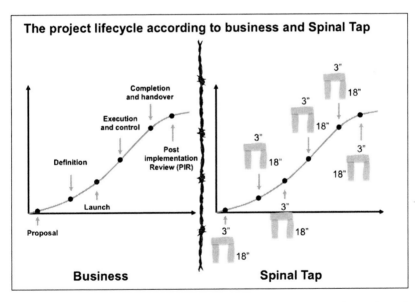

One such moment was the occasion when my friend Bill Nelson was trapped inside a perspex cage, which failed to open at the start of one of the dates from Be-Bop Deluxe's "Sunburst Finish" tour. Check out the album cover for Sunburst Finish on Google to see the picture that inspired the perspex cage sketch in Spinal Tap.

If I had a dollar for every company that has told me they have wasted millions on poorly specified projects that resulted in delivery of the wrong thing, I would have retired and you would not be reading this.

Spinal Tap business lesson # 1. If you have problems executing a project, look back several stages to the project definition. Fuzzy objectives produce fuzzy action.

Spinal Tap business lesson # 2. Project management does not have to be complex. Just following a simple process from proposal, definition, launch, execution, completion and review is better than using the back of a cigarette packet to ensure ideas turn into action.

Spinal Tap business lesson # 3. Details matter if you want something to be right first time. They are not just for nerds.

I had my own Spinal Tap moment when I made a large investment of money and time in 'cult punk rocker and two hit wonder' John Otway's World Tour. This was a wonderful idea to live the Rock'n'Roll dream on a record-breaking world tour.

The itinerary included the greatest venues on the planet: Liverpool's Cavern, on to New York's Carnegie Hall, Caesar's

Palace, Tahiti for rest and relaxation, Sydney Opera House and the seven star Dubai Madinat Hotel and back to The Albert Hall.

So this was an audacious aspiration. Two weeks circumventing the world, living la vida loca, a birth, a death and a car crash, but not necessarily in that order! In case you are not familiar with John Otway, he brands himself as a 'microstar' and 'two-hit wonder' in a world more usually populated by one hit wonders. More details on the strange and wonderful John Otway at the Academy of Rock website.

The idea was effectively 'the real Spinal Tap tour' and there are plenty of people who would like to live the Rock'n'Roll dream for two weeks, so what went wrong? Well, the project definition stage was omitted in favour of going straight from a broad idea to launch. This meant that nobody had a clue what was happening and how their activity related to the overall plan. Poor execution of the strategy killed the project dead. The tour eventually breathed its last breath due to cash flow starvation to pay Air Tahiti for the Airbus 340 we had hired. That said, it was one of the more comedic projects I've ever been called in to rescue. By the time John Otway called for my help, it was already too late and despite injecting a small fortune of my personal savings into the project and providing 4 months full time help, my mistake was in trying to help someone who I regarded as a friend. Here are just a few of the bizarre escapades that occurred en route to the lift off that never lifted off:

- John Otway turned down potential help from Sir Bob Geldof after I had initiated a dialogue. This was due to Otway's embarrassment over being turned down for a date by Bob's wife, Paula Yates some 25 years previously. Otway told her that she would never have another chance of going out with a rock star – how wrong could you be! See the back of John's book 'Rock'n'Roll's greatest failure' to see why Paula was livid with Mr Otway.

• The tour team had hired a jet that was too big to take off from the airport, creating the 'un-Rock'n'Roll itinerary'

It is the story of a man who . . .

almost rejected Pete Townshend as his producer

has never repaid a record company advance in his life

once put on a benefit concert for his own record company after they had cancelled his contract

signed himself to the mighty Warner Brothers label simply by pressing his own records with the WB logo in the middle, and

broke up with Paula Yates, telling her it was the last chance she'd get to go out with a rock star.

Cor Baby, That's Really Me! is John Otway's hilarious yet moving account of his insane assault on the music industry, a tale of blind ambition and rank incompetence, and a salutory lesson for aspiring musicians on how not to achieve greatness.

But if the John Otway story is one of failure, it is failure on a grand scale. And it makes compulsive reading too!

John Lennon Airport – Rotherham – JFK via an 'aviation expert' who John told me was "a nutter". Harsh words from a self confessed serial failure!

- The Travel Agent we engaged managed to lose half of the fully paid up passengers from the passenger list by hiking the price and sending an impersonal communication to the Otway fans, who turned against the Travel Agent and voted with their feet. The plane went from being 50% full to 25% full. The travel agent knew how to count money, but did not know much about travel nor the mind of the John Otway fan. This was a fatal error in terms of cashflow.

- We managed to book the Sydney Opera House for the very first punk rock gig in history at this venue. When I called them, we were lucky in so far as they had never heard of John Otway!

- Pop kitsch disco divas 'The Cheeky Girls' were replaced by an unknown tribute act on the 'Viva Las Vegas' punk cabaret leg of the tour. At that time The Cheeky Girls would have produced some popular media interest but John refused to have them along claiming that they 'had no talent'. This was another strange statement from a man who himself claims to be talentless! They were replaced by a roster of artists who were John's friends and essentially brought no additional passengers with them, thus we failed to fill the seats.

- We did however create some great chances to rescue sales. For example we arranged for a prime time slot on

BBC Radio with 10 million listeners. John Otway chose to 'narrowcast' to his fan base, who had already bought their tickets, rather than 'broadcasting' the real Spinal Tap tour concept to a wider set of thrillseekers. This was despite giving John considerable coaching and direct advice on handling the media. Ego is a powerful barrier to enterprise and can over-ride all rationality when life or death business decisions need to be taken.

• We also managed to persuade the President of Tahiti to host an official welcome to an ex-dustman from Aylesbury i.e. John Otway. What a great pity the plane never took off!

You can read more about the Monty Pythonesque comedy of errors that was John Otway's world tour at the Academy of

Beware of the flowers ...

and large loans ...

Peter Cook   www.academy-of-rock.co.uk

Rock website. What then are the transferable lessons for leaders, entrepreneurs and people trying to do new things?

Spinal Tap business lesson # 4. Inspiration is essential for innovation, but perspiration is even more important to turn your ideas into profit! Bright ideas are plentiful but people who are prepared to sweat it out are rarer.

Spinal Tap business lesson # 5. Creative people may not like accountancy but lack of cash flow kills dreams. Quit dreaming and get on the spreadsheet.

Spinal Tap business lesson # 6. Always listen to your wife. They can see all.

"Knowledge speaks but wisdom listens"

Jimi Hendrix

A Night at the Opera

I spent a night at the opera recently, when we went to see Rusalka, by Dvorak. In brief Rusalka develops the fairy story of a mermaid, who longs to leave her underwater kingdom. She falls in love with a handsome prince but must pay the price of losing her voice. Of course the opera ends in tragedy. Sounds innocent enough? Well, readers of the UK newspaper The Daily Telegraph were outraged due to the modern adaptation, which recasts the mermaid as a hooker and the wicked witch as a brothel madam – pretty much Sex, Opera and Rock'n'Roll but we'll leave that for another book!

Sex, Opera and Rock'n'Roll aside, I was fascinated to watch the workings of the orchestra during the three hour performance. There's no room for free improvisation in such a setting, with up to 40 people performing together, alongside a similar number of people on stage. The role of the orchestra conductor is pivotal as the main communication medium between stage and orchestra pit. It's an idea I have drawn parallels about in the book "Sex, Leadership and Rock'n'Roll". Quite by chance, I ended up having a conversation with Andy Wooler, an orchestral brass player, big band jazz fiend, conductor, music fanatic and Academy Technology Manager at Hitachi Data Systems.

What parallel business lessons can businesses learn from a night at the opera?

Size matters – It may be easy to jam in a small group where the task is simple, but once group size gets beyond a certain number and the task becomes complex, co-ordination of tasks is required if the music is to come out to the same quality standard on a consistent basis. In an orchestra this is accomplished by the use of sheet music and a conductor. In business, this may be achieved through procedures, standards and/or supervision and guidance. I've discussed these ideas before via the Music – Business mix:

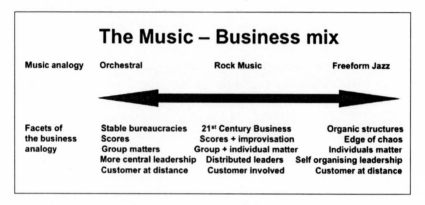

The Music – Business mix

Music analogy	Orchestral	Rock Music	Freeform Jazz

| Facets of the business analogy | Stable bureaucracies
Scores
Group matters
More central leadership
Customer at distance | 21st Century Business
Scores + improvisation
Group + individual matter
Distributed leaders
Customer involved | Organic structures
Edge of chaos
Individuals matter
Self organising leadership
Customer at distance |

Beauty and the Beast – What is often heard in an opera are the highlights/melodies. Yet, these rest on what my PhD music teacher friend calls the 'boring bits'. Without a number of pieces of substructure music does not always have grace and beauty. In the pop music world, take a listen to some of the hidden arrangements in The Beatles work circa Sgt. Pepper or Bohemian Rhapsody by Queen to hear what I mean.

Innovation and the Opera – Andy points out that, despite what conventional wisdom might suggest, there is room for innovation in the opera. Specifically, innovation manifests itself in two ways:

• **The choice of conductor** – For example, Leonard Bernstein transformed the music of many works such as Romeo and Juliet, where he changed the story and added music.

Bernstein was regarded as an eclectic composer, fusing jazz, Jewish music, and the work of other classical composers, such as Stravinsky. A kind of Jimi Hendrix of the classics.

- **The storyline/staging** – The other area where innovation occurs in opera is in the storyline. Andy recalls seeing "The Last Supper' at Glyndebourne, where Judas was included in the guest list at a Last Supper reunion. Another example is the recasting of "The Marriage of Figaro" in the 1960s. The transformation of Rusalka towards a more modern interpretation is just such an example of changing the setting to engage a new audience, even if Daily Telegraph readers were not amused!

In conclusion, superb performance often rests on a number of invisible substructures. Structure is not the enemy of creativity. Graceful performance in any field is often the product of a great deal of structure, some of which is non-obvious. A conversation with Nigel Kennedy confirms these observations and there is more in the article on Kennedy's genius later on in this book.

Andy Wooler may be contacted on Twitter @awooler and via www.andywooler.info/wordpress

"The essence of strategy is choosing what not to do"

Michael Porter

Magic Bullets

 Tom Peters retweeted you   Oct 6

Oct 6: ⬤TWalk ⬤tom_peters If there were any magic bullets they
would have all been fired ...

Tom Peters, world class author, speaker and thinker kindly retweeted the above comment, which I thought up in the shower. So many times in business, we expect there to be a magic bullet to solve our problems, yet this is rare. So, in a deep sense of irony, here are five of my own MBBs - that's a TLA (Three Letter Acronym – I just hate abbreviations!:-) for "Magic Business Bullets":

 To solve a complex business problem, seek to understand it in detail first, then examine alternative options before reaching for a "solution"

 If you want change to take root, plant seeds by involving people - good participation breeds commitment, dictation breeds compliance

 The real skill of making new things happen at work is in the development and execution of the strategy rather than at the strategy creation stage

 More data does not always equate to more intelligence or wisdom

 There are no magic bullets in business

Best fit succeeds over best practice in a complex and changing world ...

www.academy-of-rock.co.uk   Peter Cook

There's plenty of business advice out there. The wise leader looks at the advice, considers the context of their business and then adapts the advice if it is appropriate, so that it best fits the business. It's IBM's original one-word motto from the turn of the 20th Century, reworked by Aretha Franklin more recently:

"Think"
Aretha Franklin and IBM

Finally, here's some of Tom Peters' thinking on some magic bullets for people leading companies. Check out Tom's work via www.tompeters.com

Leaders

- *Care*
- *Show respect to all*
- Reward people skills
- Win people over
- *Focus on intangibles*
- Teach, teach, teach
- Share leadership
- *Foster open communication*
- Create opportunities to lead
- Relish diversity
- Promote difference
- Fuel enthusiasm

"If a window of opportunity appears, don't pull down the shade"

Tom Peters

Living In The Past: Will rock reinvent itself?

Music is applied physics. Yet the beauty of music is that there are almost infinite ways of recombining notes, timbre, textures and so on. With this in mind you would think that we would expect infinite variety and a never ending supply of new music? Well, it does rather seem that the human condition is to like 'repeat performances'. Richard Strange, leader of The Doctors of Madness told me "All music is mongrel". Here are a few harsh examples of what he means, all the more so because I love many of the acts I'm about to apparently critique:

- Oasis are a 30 year later 'echo' of The Beatles.
- Bruce Springsteen is Bob Dylan speeded up.
- The Darkness are Queen without disco, vaudeville and opera.
- Britney is Madonna without the ballads and Evita.
- Prince is Hendrix fused with better lighting, song structures and superb marketing.
- Paul Weller is The Small Faces with the addition of speed.
- Gaga is Madonna, Queen, Glam all rolled into one and presented with superb theatricals.
- Uptown Funk by Bruno Mars is a clever synthesis of Prince's music and Michael Jackson's dance routines.

This principle also transfers to classical music. Listen to the middle section of the classic glam rock song "Blockbuster" by The Sweet. This is borrowed shamelessly from the end of a piece of Bach or Mozart. Note for the musicians out there: The middle section uses the 5th to the 1st interval to produce

Peter Cook   www.academy-of-rock.co.uk

an authentic cadence, reminiscent of many consonant classical symphonies.

Why, then, do we enjoy what I call 'karaoke' performances? It's a question I've wondered about over the years and I suspect it could be as simple as the fact that they remind us of our youth and the music we have become familiar with. As Kate Bush so wisely put it:

"Every old sock needs an old shoe"
Kate Bush – "Moments of Pleasure" from "The Red Shoes"

A parallel idea is that in new product innovation, the probability of success is dramatically improved if the new product is a development of something we are familiar with.

But do we have to repeat ourselves? Is the future of music hopeless? Can rock reinvent itself? Well, in some cases, the answer to this final question is yes.

Radiohead's album "Kid A" is a good example of bold reinvention in an industry that encourages repetition. Faced with an enormous success from their previous album "OK Computer", it would have been tempting to rewrite this album.

Instead they adopted a completely different approach, which admittedly was not as successful, but seems not to have hurt them in the long run. There are previous echoes of this bold behaviour in the form of Pink Floyd's follow up to "Dark Side Of The Moon". "Wish You Were Here" was a non-obvious follow up to this classic album.

Conclusions: Will rock reinvent itself?

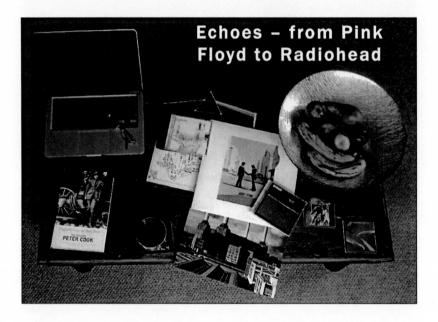

Echoes – from Pink Floyd to Radiohead

Although pop and rock music quite literally devours itself in many cases, there is hope in the form of people that don't see life as a repeat performance.

Companies can learn parallel lessons by adopting a mindset that looks to the future whilst respecting cultural signifiers of the past, if they want to traverse generational boundaries in the sale of their new products. We look at examples of great reinventors in Part 4 of this book, via the medium of Madonna, David Bowie and Bill Nelson.

Peter Cook   www.academy-of-rock.co.uk

"The past is only the future with the lights on"

Blink 182

I Predict a Riot: The Kaiser Chiefs and new business models

Tim Kastelle, Lecturer in Innovation Management for The University of Queensland Business School noticed a piece of innovation in The Kaiser Chiefs' album "The Future is Medieval", which focuses on the idea of mass personalisation. He takes up the story.

I just finished listening to my version of the new album by The Kaiser Chiefs, "The Future is Medieval", and I have to say that I'm pretty happy with it. You may well ask what makes it my version?

The thing that makes it mine is that I picked the 10 songs to go on it, I picked the order they'd go in, and I made the artwork. And I guess I'm promoting it now too, even though what I'm really interested in is the business model. Here is how Mike Masnick describes the idea:

> *"...there are two key things that the band is doing with this digital (and its only digital) release: Let fans create a 'custom' album with custom artwork. The band is effectively releasing 20 songs, and users get to pick which 10 they want, and put them in any order they want — and then they get a custom piece of album artwork, based on the choices. The website is fun to play around with as well.*
>
> *Then, once you've bought the album, you also get a 'fan page' for the unique album that you created, and if you*

drive others to that page and they buy the copy of the album that you created, you get £1 (the full album costs £7.50)".

I'm curious to see how it will work. Masnick has some reservations about the choices that they've made, but it illustrates an important point. When you face a turbulent environment, as record labels certainly do at the moment, then you have to experiment with new business models to find out what works. This is an interesting experiment.

Here is what singer Ricky Wilson had to say about it:

"We're quite excited about this. Why not make an album yourself? We wanted to reward the fans for being our fans and thought this could be nice.

We just sold all our tickets for our first two gigs exclusively on our Facebook page, which worked a treat and we're going to be getting fans to use Facebook polls to help us pick set-lists and stuff. Goodness knows if it will work. We've used a load of our own money to hire some really clever people to build the site and market it so we're hopeful. This definitely isn't some sort of two-fingers-to-the-system thing. In fact our label Fiction have been very supportive. It's not supposed to be a massive statement to the world or a fight against anything. It was just fun and we needed that to be honest".

This strategy is similar to that pursued by Procter & Gamble, who are regarded as experts in open innovation. This is evident in the following ways:

1. P&G have extensive research networks (both proprietary and open ones) that regularly lead to the development of new ideas.
2. The percentage of patents in use in products has increased from less than 10% to better than 50%. Just think what the impact of that is on P&G's ability to generate returns on its ideas.
3. Their new product success rate has increased from 35% to better than 50%. Again, this is a substantial improvement in performance.
4. The percentage of new P&G products that include elements developed outside of the firm has increased from 15% to over 35%. Innovation that comes from the marketplace is less expensive and is already partly market tested for early adoption.

So what's different in the case of The Kaiser Chiefs from a business model standpoint?

1. By getting people involved it changes the value proposition pretty significantly. If you take an hour to put together your own version of the CD, then you're likely to feel pretty invested in it. In my case, that worked pretty well because, even though I love and have bought a couple of Kaiser Chiefs songs, this is the first full CD of theirs that I've ever gotten.
2. The value network is different too, with fans promoting the record. By involving the end user in the profits, it may assist in stopping people from downloading the product

for free. All the customers are shareholders.

3.   It's also interesting to see what hasn't changed – the value chain that produced the record is pretty standard.

The band was supported by their label to go into the studio to make the music, and all the rest of the process right up to distribution is pretty standard. So it's not a full DIY value chain like Kristin Hersh is using.

I have no idea if this will work or not. But in a sense it doesn't matter, because once it's done, we'll know something about this type of approach. And other bands and labels can try it themselves, or come up with a way to make this business model better.

The one thing that I do know is that if your business model is in trouble, trying out ideas that engage your customers is probably smarter than suing them.

Tim Kastelle is Lecturer in Innovation Management for The University of Queensland Business School. He may be contacted at www.timkastelle.org

"Strategy is a pattern in a stream of decisions"

Henry Mintzberg

Crowdfunding Strategy

The World Wide Web has its fans and critics, but undeniably the phenomenon known as crowdfunding would simply not be possible without the internet. Crowdfunding brings together people from all over the globe who share a passion for a project and who are prepared to invest in that project ahead of its realisation, to make it possible. This helps entrepreneurs kick start projects that would otherwise not be possible by conventional means. Crowdfunding is increasingly being used as a strategy for collaboration between people who share nothing else in common other than a collective passion to make something new happen and contributes to innovation through the power of collaboration. The approach is risk free for the people who back a project as nothing is paid if the project does not reach its financial target.

I was privileged to play a part in helping two musicians successfully fund their crowdfunding projects. The first for an album and UK tour for Bernie Tormé, former lead guitar player for Ozzy Osbourne and Deep Purple's Ian Gillan. The other for the Godfather of Punk, Richard Strange, who has mounted an audacious arts project to celebrate the life and works of American novelist William Burroughs. So, what has Crowdfunding done in these two examples?

Hard Rock Café

Bernie Tormé's project was funded via Pledge Music and was so popular that it was fully funded within 24 hours and subsequently funded itself to 420% of its original goal. This has enabled the artist to invest more in the album production and provide additional benefits to the people who pledged their support.

Beyond fundraising, crowdfunding has reconnected Bernie and his music with his community of fans across the world. He says that crowdfunding has been developed a real community spirit compared with the old music business model where a record company puts the record out and there is no connection between the artist and the consumer. The crowd are now helping him to market his UK Tour, having made the financial and emotional commitment to the album project.

Collaboration is key to such projects, building online communities who spread the word via social media, to find the needles in the haystack around the world, people who want to get involved in the project but otherwise would not know about it. Collaboration also featured in the build up to the project. Bernie gave his backers exclusive access to the writing and making of the album via video and other updates.

A little bit of pizazz also helps ... In Tormé's case, he auctioned his Fender Stratocaster guitar which was given to him by Ozzy Osbourne to create an aspirational goal for the project. Since Bernie did not really want to sell the guitar and because it was donated by the Prince of Darkness, he set the price at £66 600!

Bernie was extremely kind in giving me some credit for helping to kick start the project and I ended up with a credit for this "accidental coaching", alongside Arthur Brown, the man behind the 1960s hit phenomenon "Fire" from The Crazy World of Arthur Brown.

Peter Cook   www.academy-of-rock.co.uk

Strangeways here we come

The Ozzy Strat: 1964 Lake Placid Blue Fender Stratocaster + AccessPass   ✕

"And this is the Strat that Ozzy gave me . . ."

£66,600
Change Currency

Richard Strange is the enigmatic founder of The Doctors of Madness, a band that inspired The Sex Pistols in their brief but riotous career. Richard was dubbed "The Godfather of Punk" as a result. He used Kickstarter to raise £10 000 from 68 crowdfunders as seed capital to fund an arts project to celebrate the life and works of William Burroughs at the Royal Festival Hall. The show featured contributions from Bill Nelson (Be-Bop Deluxe), Sarah Jane Morris (The Communards), Audrey Riley (Smashing Pumpkins, Muse, Kate St. John (Philip Glass, Marianne Faithfull), a one-off reunion of The Doctors of Madness and many others. Richard sees crowdfunding as means of democratising the music business. He observes:

> *"Ideas are the real currency. No, strike that. Ideas are the ONLY currency. Music should describe the energy of ideas. If it's wrong, make it brilliantly wrong and you get it right. When you're stuck, bang together two existing ideas and you'll spark something new. Whatever you do, Don't Whinge!"*

Crowdfunding Strategy summed up

Crowdfunding works on some time-honoured principles:

- Collaborate via a crowdfunding platform to find the 'long tail' of backers who share a passion in your project.

- Build your online community by conveying the essence of the project in a potent way.

- Communicate with your community frequently to build commitment and develop your network.

- Deliver your promises along the way and engage more backers through the power of the crowd.

"Music is all recombinant DNA.
It is just banging two existing
rocks together and seeing
what spark is produced"

Richard Strange

Selling England By The Pound: Andrew Sentance on financial strategy

Dr. Andrew Sentance is Senior Economic Adviser to PricewaterhouseCoopers and combines a demanding career with a love of classic rock music. He was appointed to an important group advising The Chancellor of the Exchequer in the UK – which was known as 'the seven wise men' plus nearly nine years at British Airways, as their Chief Economist. I discovered that Andrew had written papers about Led Zeppelin, Genesis and the economy – I had to find out more:

"Mervyn King, the Governor of the Bank of England, is a big sports fan and puts a lot of sporting analogies in his speeches. He once explained monetary policy by referring to Maradona's second goal against England in the 1986 World Cup semi-final. I am useless at sport but I really enjoy rock music. So when I joined the Monetary Policy Committee of the Bank of England, I felt there was an opportunity to make some connections between rock music and economics.

In the summer of 2010, I started to argue for higher interest rates and I was looking for a good title for the first speech in which I would explain my position. The speech was in Reading, with its connections to the Reading Festival.

I came up with the title, 'How long should the song remain the same?', based on the title of the Led Zeppelin album. The basis of my argument was that very low interest rates had been put in place to deal with a crisis in 2008/9, but the economy had started to recover and inflation had been much higher than expected. So interest rate policy should not remain the same when the economy was changing. You can read the speech on the Bank of England website.

I went on to give another speech with a rock music theme in February 2011, inspired by the Genesis album, 'Selling England By The Pound', also available on the Bank of England website.

I find that since music is a fairly global language, that the use or adaptation of a classic rock album title is a great way to get people's attention for important subjects, especially if the content is a bit dry. At the same time, you are essentially

limited to a few words for a rock song, so it forces you to be economical in your choice of words. That matters a lot for busy people."

I wanted to know how this went down in the corridors of power so I asked Andrew to reflect on his musical life.

"Most people enjoy music. And many people in my generation appreciate the classic rock of the 1970s. So music is often a good icebreaker for conversations at business lunches, dinners and meetings.

I've found many rock music enthusiasts in my business contacts and at the highest levels in the Bank of England and at the Treasury. Great rock music is the combination of individual virtuoso performances and the ability to work together as a band. This is one of the key lessons I take away from the rock world for my career. The combination of individual ability and team effort is at the heart of success not just in the world of music, but also in business and politics. For the dominant and mercurial lead guitarist, read the overbearing CEO or Prime Minister who does not acknowledge and recognise the views of his/her colleagues. All are ultimately doomed – notwithstanding their ability.

To succeed in rock music, you need to be good, but you also need to be surrounded by other good musicians and be able to work constructively and creatively with them for the good of the band. When this works well, great music results. That is the approach I find works well in the business context too."

I look forward to more titles informing economic strategy:

- Can't buy me love.
- One vision, one spreadsheet.
- Stairway to fiscal union.

Contact Andrew via his blog www.sentance.com

"I want everything louder than everything else"

Deep Purple on strategy

PART 2 – Creativity

Introduction to Part 2 – Creativity

Most businesses are interested in innovation, yet they are much less interested in creativity. Simply stated, innovation is the output, creativity is the input. So, if you have no creativity, you have no innovation. Nonetheless, most businesses want the kind of creativity that converts into innovation rather than the type beloved of artists and some musicians sitting in their attics and basements making art and music purely for their own pleasure. There's nothing wrong with that but, let's be clear, creativity in business without appropriateness is merely art for arts sake.

We look at a number of approaches and tools for practical creativity in this part of the book. We start with the notion that creativity and structure are bedfellows, using the examples of Deep Purple and lessons from jazz to inform our thinking. We examine personal creative style via the comparison of Jimi Hendrix and Eric Clapton, who offer a stark contrast in terms of their approach to creativity in music.

Constraints are surprisingly a spur to creativity and we examine the theory of constraints via the example of Jack White, Brian Eno and some business examples, including the introduction of the first treatment for AIDS which was brought to market in record time spurred on by constraints.

Creativity at work requires a set of underpinning values if it is to take root. The Beatles offer us insights into a model approach to make new ideas part of the normal fabric of business life. We then examine the role of creativity techniques and tools via a post on Brian Eno's Oblique Strategies. This is followed by a true creativity giant in the form of Michael Michalko, author of Thinkertoys, Cracking Creativity and many other books on the art and methodologies that make creativity reliable.

For a bit of light relief, I have added a mini article containing ten top business tips from a creative adaptation of pop and rock songs. This is bite-size learning if you are in a hurry or have no tolerance for business consultancy jargon. There's much more like this in the book "Punk Rock People Management".

We have a masterclass in creativity from Scott McGill, jazz-fusion guitarist who has studied at the feet of jazz masters. He offers us the insight that both formal learning and intuition are valuable when coming up with new ideas, seeing everything he learns as a 'playground' for new ideas.

That said, creativity does not have to come down to brainstorming techniques. Sometimes ideas come naturally as per the story of "Two Pints of Lager and a Packet of Crisps, Please". The punk/D.I.Y. ethos is echoed and developed by punk marketer Richard Laermer, who, in common with Steve Jobs, favours intuitive approaches to market research and marketing over endless measurement.

So, there we have it. A veritable cornucopia of thought leadership on creativity with parallel lessons for business and individuals alike. Take a walk on the wild side …

"Imagination is more important than knowledge"

Albert Einstein
Full time physicist and dreamer
Part time musician and mathematician

Deep Purple In Rock: Improvisation and discipline in business

The hard rock band Deep Purple are responsible for millions of young boys camping out in music shops trying to play the riff to "Smoke on the Water". At the age of 14 I used to sit atop the stairs at home in the darkness trying to figure out the riff to the song with my Hofner Futurama guitar and 10 Watt Zenta amp, until my mum would shout me to come down to get my fish finger sandwiches. Aside from these personal problems, Deep Purple offer us a great example of improvisation and discipline in the context of a rock outfit.

The Mark II incarnation of the band is generally considered to be perhaps the definitive line up, but also the most volatile.

www.academy-of-rock.co.uk   Peter Cook

Much of the conflict within Deep Purple arose between the singer Ian Gillan and Ritchie Blackmore, their phenomenal virtuoso guitarist and moody maverick.

Have a look at Deep Purple in action. Especially some of their early work on YouTube such as "Mandrake Root" or "Wring That Neck". You can actually see Blackmore sending musical instructions (using his arms as a baton!) to the keyboard player Jon Lord, to repeat and develop certain lines. He also uses quite aggressive movements with the neck of his guitar to tell the rhythm section (Ian Paice and Roger Glover) when to start and stop within the music. What parallel lessons may we learn for business from Deep Purple?

Deep Purple innovation lesson # 1. Innovation needs discipline and structure.

Paradoxically, innovation in business requires discipline as much as it does creativity: Creativity to come up with novel strategies; Discipline to execute them, so that ideas turn into profitable innovations. Companies such as Google and Innocent may seem to be all about creativity at first glance, but a deeper inspection reveals discipline and structure, even if that structure does not emanate from management in all cases. Giving people 20% of their time to work on speculative projects is the business equivalent of a free form jam within "Space Truckin'", "Lazy", "Mistreated" and many other pieces of Deep Purple's repertoire. To read more on this point check out the article 'The 3Rs of Leadership' later on in this book.

Deep Purple innovation lesson # 2. Diverse teams require strong leadership.

Paradox number two is that it requires extremely strong leadership and a compelling shared vision to hold diverse people together. A rock band often contains an extremely diverse mixture of people by design, which is why they often have dysfunctional lives as teams. Yet they cannot produce a product without each other. In Deep Purple's case we have two mercurial figures in the form of singer Ian Gillan and guitar player Ritchie Blackmore. These were held in balance by the amiable bass player, Roger Glover, the delightfully genial Ian Paice on drums and the man who taught me to love the organ, Jon Lord, R.I.P. Somewhat strangely, Deep Purple align quite well with my own experience in bands. There is a direct relationship between the people at the back of the stage and the higher level human competences of humility and so on ...

By the same token, to encourage a company of diverse people that continuously learn/adapt and improvise into the future requires leadership that is precise on the destination, yet loose on the journey.

Deep Purple innovation lesson # 3. Unity needs conflict.

Conflict will occur and it must be handled properly if progress is to be made in an innovative enterprise. Ultimately Blackmore's maverick behaviour proved too much for the band, especially

the singer Ian Gillan, and despite several reunions, the band proved impossible to hold together. Thomas and Killman (good name for conflict gurus by the way) identified five things we can do about conflict:

1. Avoid – just walk away physically or emotionally.
2. Accommodate – smooth things over for others.
3. Compromise – reach a low level solution for all.
4. Problem-solve – reach a high level solution for all.
5. Compete – play to win.

Peter Cook   www.academy-of-rock.co.uk

To resolve conflict, all five postures may be used to produce results. Some companies just like some individuals major on just a few of these. Contrary to popular business speak, this cannot always be win-win, nor need it be lose-lose. No-lose strategies are often overlooked as a viable alternative to win-win bargaining. It's what my football fanatic friends call a nil-nil draw. Successful conflict handlers are also great at separating conflict over issues from conflict over people and personalities. They are also highly creative and willing to come up with options, especially when things seem deadlocked.

Who knows, with better management to hold the creative tensions together, Deep Purple Mark II may have lasted longer, produced even better material and I would have had even more medieval rock riffs to learn!

"I have learned throughout my life as a composer chiefly through my mistakes and pursuits of false assumptions, not by my exposure to founts of wisdom and knowledge"

Igor Stravinsky

The Flow: Personal mastery in business and all that jazz

Mastery, unconscious competence, effortless genius. These are all ways to describe what Mihaly Csikszentmihalyi called the state of 'flow'. Sports people refer to flow as being 'in the zone' and Madonna calls it "Into the Groove". What can we learn about flow from music that we can transfer to the world of business and personal development?

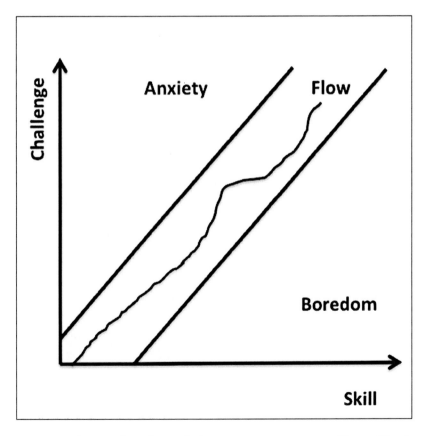

www.academy-of-rock.co.uk   Peter Cook

To experience the state of flow take a look at some masters of their craft operating at a state of effortless genius. Have a look at Joe Pass, Prince, Wes Montgomery or Barney Kessel on YouTube.

What then is flow? What can we learn about effortless mastery from professional musicians? I interviewed John Howitt, a professional session musician, who has performed with Celine Dion, Anastasia and Shirley Bassey. He also works with us in our business and music master classes. As a session musician, John must be at peak performance with every engagement. I asked him to reveal some of his tips for staying in the flow:

John: "Mastery comes out of preparation. In business circles, people talk of the need for 10 000 hours disciplined practice to master an art or discipline.

Contrary to what amateur musicians might think, to do what I do, it's all about practice and preparation. I have probably exceeded the 10 000 hours in my career as a session musician and still spend 5 hours a day playing an instrument if I am not actually engaged in a piece of client work".

Peter: Many so-called 'creatives' say that they feel they would lose their creativity/mojo if they over prepared. What do you say to that?

John: "Practice gives you ease AND versatility. Playing routine pieces of music almost goes on auto pilot allowing you to concentrate on what is needed to add that extra piece of sparkle.

This is just as applicable to business and personal excellence as it is to performing music".

Peter: As well as your stage and session work, I know you also record soundtrack music for films. In your experience, how do you move from a performance role to one that is perhaps more introverted?

John: "In one way, there is no difference. When performing, you still need to keep your focus both internally on the mastery of what you are doing, whilst keeping your antennae open to hear those around you.

It's what the business gurus called 'emotional intelligence' – living inside your own head AND paying attention to your co-performers. Good musicians and leaders do both. Bad musicians and leaders just listen to themselves.

That said, when I'm recording soundtracks, I can focus completely in on the point of detail that I'm working with, PLUS keep in mind the overall piece. The big picture AND the small detail are essential if you are to achieve what Peter Senge calls personal mastery. As a musician or leader, I find it essential to be both gregarious AND solitary".

Peter: Please share some insights on innovation for us?

John: "In music, the innovation challenge lies in breaking away from habits. Practice can force you into habit but it need not. It's what companies like Nokia and firstdirect have achieved, rather than just repeating themselves. In particular firstdirect are unique in the banking world as they do not work from algorithms when handling customer enquiries by phone. Instead, they hire people that are great listeners, who are interested in other people's problems and who are expert problem solvers. These are also part of the repertoire of great session musicians.

There are many stories of firstdirect going the extra mile to serve customers. As far as I know, it's the only bank that people talk about using the word 'love' in the same sentence as the word 'bank'.

Furthermore, "There are no mistakes", as Miles Davis says. If you want to run an innovative enterprise, you must be prepared to accommodate occasional mistakes and even failures, just like the very best music acts. Sometimes mistakes make

Professors of Rock'n'Roll Business: John Howitt is joined by Professor Dennis Tourish and Peter Cook at a Business meets Music masterclass

great music, such as the theme from Jaws, which arose from taking two notes that are essentially dissonant, which creates the tension in the build up of the piece".

John Howitt and I offer masterclasses in personal mastery, using a suite of high-level psychological constructs blended with musical interludes and audience participation if you are 'in the flow'.

"Music gives a soul to the universe, wings to the mind, flight to the imagination and life to everything"

Plato

Creative Style: Hendrix vs. Clapton

Jimi Hendrix is still considered to be one of the greatest guitar players in the world, more than 40 years after his premature death in 1970. Plenty of guitarists have surpassed Hendrix in sheer technical dexterity, but most people point towards Hendrix's 'attitude' towards the instrument as the source of his genius rather than his technical skill per se. In my own case, my life was never the same after I saved up the money to buy a copy of his hit single "Purple Haze", which I still own.

Firestarters – Bernie Tormé and Peter Cook recreate Jimi Hendrix's guitar sacrifice

Talking to Bernie Tormé, guitarist for Ozzy Osbourne and Deep Purple's Ian Gillan confirms the view that Hendrix had more than just guitar technique:

> *"For me, Jimi Hendrix epitomises innovation in rock music still. His willingness to explore sounds that were way beyond those being used by his contemporaries at the time*

still stands up to scrutiny. He had a playground approach to using equipment and effects that was totally alien at the time. He also fused styles in ways that others would not dream of".

Check out Hendrix's classic performance of "The Star Spangled Banner" on YouTube from Woodstock in 1969 to hear the master at work. I staged a re-enactment of Hendrix's famous guitar burning stunt at a University in Cambridge during an Executive MBA programme. You can find more pictures in our book "Sex, Leadership and Rock'n'Roll". Here's one to whet your appetite:

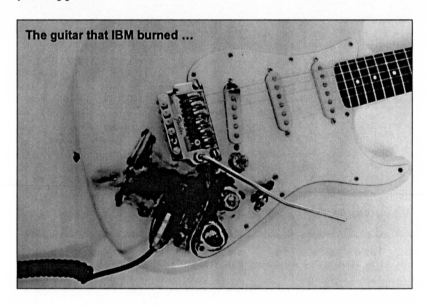

The guitar that IBM burned ...

Hendrix is an archetype of what psychologist Professor Michael Kirton would call an innovator, someone who fused together musical ideas to come up with something totally novel. Jimi Hendrix fused the blues with soul, funk, hard rock and psychedelia in a heady cocktail, whereas many musicians stay within a musical genre. Some might say that he lost some of his audience in the process, if you were to take a very critical view of his work.

So what about Eric Clapton then? Generally speaking, Eric Clapton has stayed within the blues genre, sticking closer to this genre and consequentially bringing it to a wider audience. This is the behaviour of what Professor Kirton calls an adaptor. In business, adaptors often have greater success than innovators, as they tend to produce ideas that are less challenging and which are recognised by consumers in the marketplace as being a logical build on existing ideas. It's the new saying, "Familiarity breeds repeat purchases".

Often we need both innovators and adaptors to produce sustainable innovations. The innovators to produce the hard-to-copy ideas and the adaptors to help bring the ideas into a practical market focus.

In business, examples of innovators include Sir Clive Sinclair, Sir Trevor Baylis and James Dyson whose innovations have not always been in tune with market desire, for example check out Dyson's early attempts to redesign the wheelbarrow (Google the ballbarrow), which failed to capture market interest. Bayliss is a particularly good example of an inventor who has produced multiple innovations, such as the Clockwork Radio. Baylis was inspired to develop this when he saw a programme about the spread of AIDS in Africa, but was met with rejection by everyone he approached until he managed to get the prototype featured on the BBC's Tomorrow's World Programme. However, many of his inventions have not succeeded.

Archetypal adaptors would include Bill Gates, Warren Buffet and possibly Sir Richard Branson, who have succeeded by taking relatively low risks with product and service innovation. Branson in particular has taken a few innovative risks, such as when he first started Virgin records. At the start of this enterprise he took on a host of unknown acts such as Gong, Henry Cow, Faust and Can. If this had continued, it is doubtful that we would have heard the name Richard Branson today. Mike Oldfield's "Tubular Bells" was a tipping point for Branson. He also gained massive publicity well beyond the size of Virgin from signing The Sex Pistols. Branson has repeated this trick several times since. For example, dressing up as a woman for the launch of Virgin Brides. Virgin gets considerably more publicity than the size of the company would dictate and this comes down to a compelling brand and the personality and public profile of its founder.

Here is the cover picture from my copy of Gong's "Camembert Electrique" album, which Branson sold for 59 pence – the same price as a single in 1974. This is a tactic that he has repeated time and time again, to disrupt tired markets.

However, we must remember that most of the Virgin empire comes from existing industries which Branson improves, such as Money, Insurance, Trains and Airlines. He is very good at spotting industries where customer service can be improved for a fair return on investment. For this reason, I'd say his approach is mostly an adaptive one like Eric Clapton. I guess someone will point out that space travel is pretty much the exception. I will report back on my return from Virgin Galactic!

"Ground control to Peter Cook"

"The spirit of jazz is the spirit of openness"

Herbie Hancock

Welcome Constraints

In the film "It Might Get Loud", guitarist Jack White says that technology makes us lazy and laziness is bad for creativity. He is right. My first guitar cost £10, the strings stood about an inch (slight exaggeration but not much) from the neck. This made my fingers work much harder to play the instrument than normal. As a result, people tell me that I can bend strings an incredible amount akin to Dave Gilmour of Pink Floyd, even though I don't use particularly a light gauge of guitar strings.

White often uses low-quality instruments to force him to play differently or work harder. He says:

> *"If it takes me three steps to get to the organ, then I'll put it four steps away. I'll have to run faster, I'll have to push myself harder to get to it."*

This is something I completely understand as a musician and a scientist. Some of the best music I made was written with just an acoustic guitar rather than a full complement of computer wizardry, or using poor equipment where there had to be some kind of struggle to extract something from it. I spent a lot of time in the 1980s and 1990s chaining reel-to-reel tape recorders together, reversing and splicing tape to create sounds that had never been heard before. Admittedly a few of these nobody ever wanted to hear again either! Brian Eno is another user of constraints as a spur to creativity, which he brought together in his "Oblique Strategies" card deck. We explore Eno's approach later on in this book.

Contrary to popular opinion, constraints are useful for creativity in all walks of life. James Dyson would not have invented the Dyson vacuum cleaner if he had not become frustrated at his vacuum cleaner, which "did not suck". Isambard Kingdom Brunel would have not built the Great Western Railway without feeling frustrated that he could not get to Cornwall quickly, and so on.

It's important to separate what I call "real constraints" from "imaginary ones". A real constraint might be a law of physics, an imaginary one simply an assumption, such as a way of doing things that has become a habit or paradigm within an industry. In my own experience, I led a team responsible for developing the world's first AIDS treatment. A real constraint was that of time. We needed to collapse the traditional drug development process time to bring the drug to market as quickly and safely as possible. At that time Wellcome was renowned for making tablet formulations and this would have been our

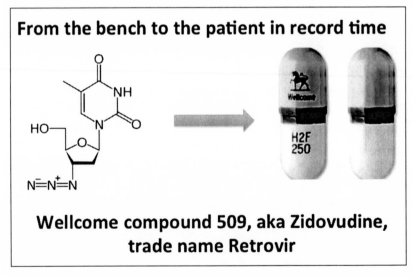

From the bench to the patient in record time

Wellcome compound 509, aka Zidovudine, trade name Retrovir

"paradigm response" to the situation. In the event, we elected to formulate the product as a capsule, something we were very inexperienced with but which would deliver the quickest route to market. This committed us to a rapid learning programme of work to develop the product. In doing so we eliminated the artificial constraint of "we always do it that way".

When we design creative thinking sessions for companies seeking to rethink their strategy, products, services and internal processes, I like to boundary the topic under study with the real constraints that surround it. These should not be too many - too many constraints tend to stifle ingenious thinking and no constraints tend to produce unfocused creativity. Some disagree with me on this, saying that creative thinking should be a "no holds barred" affair. Long experience in working with people and companies that look for commercial creativity i.e. ideas that have utility suggest that this is wasteful where a narrow search is needed. It also often does not lead to execution, as the ideas developed do not pass the obstacles that are in the way of implementation of the idea. The theory of constraints is well documented and mostly forgotten by people who think only about the positive side of business improvement. I wrote recently for Sir Richard Branson on this topic in terms of the internal barriers to innovation. Read more at www.virgin.com/author/peter-cook

For many years, I've used my "fried egg model" to describe the essentials needed to specify a problem or opportunity that is amenable to ingenious thinking. I was delighted when Charles Handy told me he had thought of something similar for his book "The Empty Raincoat" but later decided it was too fanciful. The fried egg model requires there to be enough "thinking space" between "the demands or goal" and "the constraints" to provide an arena for productive creativity - "the choices". This is why it's a fried egg and not a boiled one sliced through the middle! Here is the fried egg I always carry in my bag alongside my computer as I'm sure we all do ...

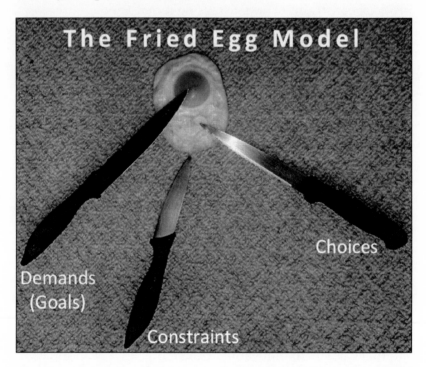

Another example of the use of constraints from the world of music comes via Arnold Schoenberg's idea of "Serialism", of which one expression is the twelve-tone technique. We wouldn't have the magnificent "Rite of Spring" without it. The technique requires that all 12 notes of the chromatic scale are sounded as often as one another whilst preventing the emphasis of any one note. This "mathematical" constraint did not get in the way of exciting music and some thought it was a breath of fresh air. Of course, as it is music, not everyone agrees!

To finish, here's that first guitar that taught me the value of constraints - I was hold it was a Hofner Futurama by the insurance salesman that sold it to me for £10. It was heavily modified with "Brian May" Burns Trisonic pickups which were its crowning glory. The guitar taught my hands to be strong! The good news today is that even cheap guitars are reasonably made in terms of playability. The aspiring musician has to find other constraints to hone their individual style and skills.

I eventually managed to buy another Hofner guitar for a similar price although his one was so bad in construction and playing that I had to take a saw to it. It was 1977 after all – the year of punk, a theme we return to shortly with Richard Laermer.

"Making the simple complicated is commonplace; making the complicated simple, awesomely simple, that's creativity"

Charlie Mingus

Creativity in business with The Beatles

A magical mystery tour of creativity

The Beatles transformed the pop song from simple three chord tales of love lost and found into an art form that has defined and redefined much popular music over the last 50 years. They also redefined the music business, retiring from touring in 1966 to spend all their time in the studio working on their art, rather than releasing albums just to increase the price of their concert tickets. Listen to "I am the Walrus" to hear one of The Beatles' more complex orchestrated pieces of psychedelic pop. Here we focus on what leaders can learn from the 3 Ds of creativity: Difference; Dissonance and Discipline. Firstly, a prologue on creativity in the arts and business.

Peter Cook   www.academy-of-rock.co.uk

Creativity in business is the thinking of novel and appropriate ideas. This differs from some forms of artistic creativity in so far as some pure artists are unconcerned with the appropriateness of their ideas. This perhaps separates The Beatles from the lone musician in their basement, who does not want or need to reach a market for their art. Innovation is therefore the successful application of those ideas. Successful music artists and businesses are as concerned with the application of their ideas as they are with their inception.

MBA creativity and innovation academic Jane Henry and Professor Charles Handy suggest that creativity in business needs four underlying principles:

- Curiosity – the systematic habit of asking great questions, testing boundaries around problems/opportunities and exploring the big picture and the detail. Artists often have this quality in great supply, business people less so.
- Love – Using a nurturing approach to leadership, participative approaches to generate ideas, and making connections between other peoples ideas to build/develop innovations.
- Forgiveness – Includes ambiguity tolerance, the encouragement of mental play and the ability to build on ideas rather than knock them down.
- A sense of direction – Having a sense of a goal or mission, an explicit or understood process for generating, improving, evaluating and implementing ideas and the ability to learn and improve. The skills of direction setting are the ones that are most important for managed creativity and often the ones most absent from artistic creativity.

The four principles and associated twelve precepts for creativity at work are summed up in this collage:

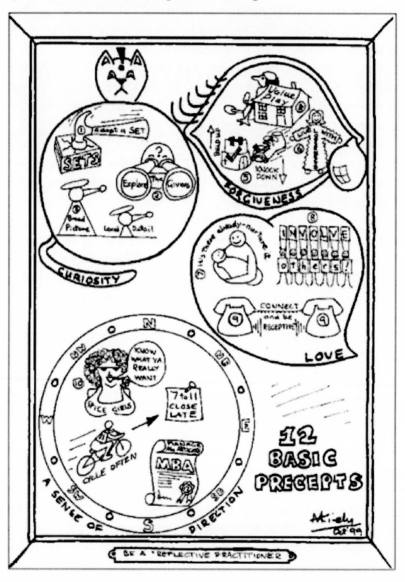

Peter Cook   www.academy-of-rock.co.uk

We now focus on the 3 Ds via The Beatles example. We will return to make the connections with Henry and Handy's principles at the end.

Creativity rests on difference

The Beatles pulled off the unusually difficult trick of making diversity work, when it is much more common to resist working with people who are different in business. Lennon and McCartney were quite different characters and this can be heard in the songs that they wrote alone. Some of Lennon's early songs are thought to have been influenced by the loss of his mother at an early age, for example "Help" and "Nowhere Man". These songs have a kind of beautiful melancholy about them. It is thought that McCartney coped with his loss rather better and tended to write more optimistic songs such as "All My Loving" and "We can Work it Out". Of course, both had their moments of doing the opposites of these – witness "Hey Jude" and "Another Day" by McCartney much later in his career. Hey Jude was intended to be a message to Lennon's son after the breakup of his marriage.

Making diversity work in business is much harder to achieve with the tendency to group similar characters together in departments or professions. However, some simple strategies such as effective job rotation, an understanding of the importance of differences and good selection methods can work wonders. It does not always come down to saturation diversity training, which is all too often used as a 'sticking plaster' for a more fundamental deficit in the enterprise.

Beatles' business lesson # I. Requisite diversity is essential if you are to have an innovative business. Find ways to resolve tensions that build up by putting different people together, but resist attempts to sidestep conflict. The creative leader utilises the tension between opposites whilst maintaining a focus on the goal.

Creativity rests on dissonance

The Beatles were pioneers at combining textures and influences from Indian music, creating a sound that was at that time dissonant to western ears.

Musical note: In music, notes are dissonant when they produce an unstable tone combination. Simply stated, they appear to grate on the ear. In the West we are mostly used to music that adopts the major, minor or blues scales. Indian music tends to use different scales to those traditionally used in Western music. Take a listen to George Harrison's song "Within You Without You" to hear what I mean.

Whilst it is possible to profit from dissonance in music, cognitive dissonance in business is a term coined by Leon Festinger, used to describe the state of holding two or more conflicting thoughts simultaneously.

Dissonance at work is the silence in the meeting when someone suggests something that is 'outside the box' of traditional thinking patterns. Sometimes it can be heard through people talking about other people as mad, bad or evil outside the meeting in the locker rooms and so on. Dissonance in business costs millions through wasted time, missed opportunities, inadequate follow-through of ideas and so on. Gerry Johnson articulated the problems associated with cognitive dissonance at work:

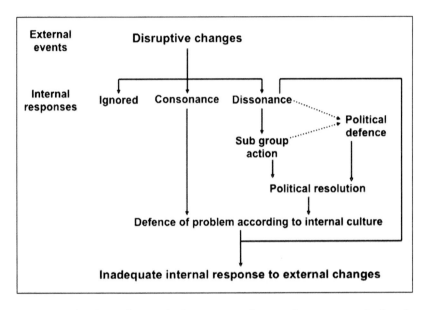

We spend a lot of time helping people use dissonance in business in order to create strategies that set businesses apart from the crowd, using a suite of divergent and convergent thinking techniques. It is a strategy that has helped companies such as Pfizer, Unilever and Johnson and Johnson to succeed, for example in their use of full figured women to promote beauty products.

www.academy-of-rock.co.uk   Peter Cook

Beatles' business lesson # 2. Find ways to listen to ideas that seem dissonant to currently accepted views of your business strategy.

Beatles' business lesson # 3. Practice curiosity on a daily basis.

Beatles' business lesson # 4. Delay evaluation of ideas for as long as possible, so that you can put distance between the novelty and a sober evaluation of the potential feasibility and impact of the idea.

Creativity rests on discipline

Contrary to conventional wisdom, creativity is not the enemy of structure and discipline. Quite the reverse. If you are going to write a song that is different, it's important to mark out the territory in ways that leads the listener towards certain familiar aspects, i.e. a refrain, verse and so on in music. Even in some of The Beatles strangest compositions, we find such devices e.g. "Strawberry Fields Forever" and "A Day In The Life".

Likewise, creativity without structure and discipline in business does not usually lead to innovation. Take the example of the pharmaceutical company Pfizer's breakthrough inhalable insulin product Exubera. The product was a brilliant idea, as it provided a 'no more needles' solution for diabetes patients. The product failed at the detailed execution stage due to the development of an inhaler that was cumbersome, difficult and something of a social embarrassment to use. Pundits suggested that it looked like a 'bong', hardly something you might get out in a restaurant to get your 'insulin hit'. Inside the company however, it seemed that nobody dared tell the CEO that the device was a 'turkey', since he had staked his own reputation and that of his employees on it. Failure to package the product in a way that 'felt familiar and comfortable' cost Pfizer an uncool $2.8 billion. That's the price of hubris, or, as Lennon and McCartney might have sung "Money (That's What I Want)".

Beatles' business lesson # 5. If innovation is your business, make sure that there is enough of 'the familiar' about the new to make the innovation attractive to your customers.

Beatles' business lesson # 6. Avoid hubris in business. It can stop you seeing what is staring you in the face.

In conclusion, The Beatles are a textbook example of Henry and Handy's business creativity principles in action:

- Curiosity – The Beatles transcended the boundaries of pop music, fusing a number of influences into their music and setting a standard that many others have followed.
- Love – Despite being opposite poles, Lennon and McCartney managed to use the creative tension between them for an extended period to produce music, which probably surpassed that which they would have produced individually.
- Forgiveness – There is considerable evidence that The Beatles used play as a means of creating for much of their

time together. Clearly this became more difficult towards the end of their life as a group.

- A sense of direction – The Beatles clearly had a purpose to be different from the norm of pop groups almost from the outset. It's probable that the 5th Beatle (George Martin) played a pivotal role in helping them execute their ideas.

Check also the interview with Professor Adrian Furnham in the leadership section of this book.

"Creativity is the sudden
cessation of stupidity"

Edwin Land

Oblique Strategies

Last year we were involved in the delivery of an innovation summit event for a major company in New York to come up with some big scale ideas to take the business forward. Obviously I am unable to discuss the company specific details of this, but I can reflect on the design process that we used to "orchestrate" creativity and innovation across the 48-hour summit.

In designing this process, we were asked to ensure that we transferred the methodologies for creativity we used to deliver the result. I decided to develop a "deck of cards" to act as a reminder for the long term, having remembered Brian Eno's "Oblique Strategies" card deck. Oblique Strategies provide a series of random "diversions" to linear thinking, much in the same way that Edward De Bono's Lateral Thinking operates. They are in effect "structures for cognitive escapology" or a set of "recipes to help you throw away the recipes". Contrary to popular thinking on the topic, creativity and discipline are bedfellows if you want your ideas to reach the market as innovations.

Eno used the Oblique Strategy cards extensively with David Bowie in his trilogy of experimental albums, "Low", "Heroes" and "Lodger". In a similar way we designed our creativity and innovation card deck to systematically move the client through the different phases required to formulate an idea, develop it, challenge it with real life constraints and devise a robust execution plan. This is quite different than turning up with a flip chart, the "rules for brainstorming" and a bucket full of hope

– one of the fatally flawed beliefs of the "let it all hang out" creativity pundits in my long experience.

EIGHT I's

IMPROVISED   ⟶ STRUCTURED

IMMENSE   ⟶ RESIZED

INCONSEQUENTIAL → MAGNIFIED

ILLEGAL   ⟶ CLEANSED

IMMORAL   ⟶ REVALUED

IMMATURE   ⟶ RETIMED

IDEALISTIC   ⟶ GROUNDED

INVENTED ELSEWHERE → CREATIVELY SWIPED

One of the provocation tools we devised

So, what have Oblique Strategies got to do with corporate creativity? Here are some of the statements from Eno's Oblique Strategy cards with parallel lessons for leaders and creativity and innovation agents:

1. State the problem in words as clearly as possible

The key move when facilitating a summit of this nature is to get a clear definition of the topic under investigation. Contrary to what most people think, unfocused brainstorming produces unfocused ideas, most of which are unlikely to convert to viable and sustainable innovations. That said, a suitable problem or opportunity must have sufficient "space" within it to allow for divergent thinking. It's what I call "specifically vague". See also the chapter on constraints and creativity earlier in this book. Time spent defining and redefining the problem is time well spent and can on occasions lead to answers without even requiring the brainstorming phase.

2. Try faking it!

Some good creativity strategies have as their subtext the use of fantasy and projection as their modus operandi, for example Superheroes, Synectics, The Disney Creativity Strategy, Dialectical approaches and so on. The act of seeing the problem or opportunity from a different viewpoint is a valuable tool in assisting people to see old topics with fresh eyes.

3. Honour thy error as a hidden intention

Some creativity methodologies have as their subtext, the introduction of random "errors" as a means of distorting frames of thinking. For example, approaches such as "Bisociation" are based on force fitting **unrelated stimuli** into the problem. As well as deliberate errors introduced by such approaches, it is important to celebrate accidental errors as new ways of finding an answer to a complex problem. Here's one of the cards from the deck we made for the event on "bisociation" and using unrelated stimuli:

4. Work at a different speed

Eno's curious advice has some rigour in terms of the background thinking behind it. When we change speed, we think differently. My co-conspirator in Canada, Ben Weinlick of The Think Jar Collective, points out that, during creative moments, the left frontal cortex experiences comparatively more sluggish activity. Unlike intelligence, creativity tends to thrive when thinking slows down. So, sometimes, slow reflection is more productive than quickfire creativity and pace is one of my key principles when designing creativity and innovation events.

Our card deck differs from the Oblique Strategy deck in several specific ways:

- We also focused on the convergent thinking step without ideas tend not to gain traction in companies. Con-

MISFITS

AKA BISOCIATION

- GO FOR A SHORT WALK OR GET HOLD OF A CATALOGUE OR MAGAZINE

- PICK SOME RANDOM OBJECTS

- MAKE ASSOCIATIONS BETWEEN THE ITEMS AND THE TOPIC AT HAND

vergence with care is a key skill in such events, perhaps more difficult than the divergent step as it's possible to lose all the value of your divergence if this is not handled appropriately.

- Our deck was customised to the industry and indeed the types of people present who were predominantly analytical in outlook.
- The deck was accompanied by expert facilitation to ensure that the necessary "climate" was developed for divergence and convergent thinking. For more on climate, see the article "Something in the Air" in Part 3 of this book.

"Build a bridge between melody and dissonance"

Bill Nelson

A Kind of Magic: Michael Michalko on creativity

Michael Michalko started his life in the military, organising groups of NATO, U.S. Army, CIA intelligence specialists and European academics who were interested in coming up with new ideas and new ways of doing things. He later applied these creative-thinking techniques to problems in the corporate world with outstanding successes with clients including DuPont, Kellogg's, Microsoft, Exxon, General Motors, Gillette, plus associations and governmental agencies around the world. Living in Rochester, NY and talking to me in Rochester UK, we conducted an online dialogue about creativity.

What do you consider the most important things companies and individuals need to do to encourage greater levels of creativity?

The most important thing for companies and individuals to understand is no that there is no such thing as failure. Failure is only a word that human beings use to judge a given situation. The artificial judgments of failure only keep you from trying something and erring or making a mistake. Yet those mistakes and errors are the way we learn and the way we grow.

As an infant, before you were educated and conditioned by others, you learned how to walk by trial and error. Suppose as infants we had learned to fear failure. Many of us would still be crawling around on all fours.

Editor's note: See also the article on glorious failure and my part in John Otway's World Tour failure, which cost me a cool £50 000 plus six months of my life trying to turn round an enterprise which needed significant help. We also look at the 'Chumbawamba effect' later on in the book with respect to entrepreneurial resilience.

Yes, it is the same with everything in life. Rather than judging something a failure, ask "What have I learned about what doesn't work?", "Can this explain something that I didn't set out to explain?", "What can I do with these results?", and "What have I discovered that I didn't set out to discover?"

Failure is a prerequisite to invention. Take the first airplane. On Dec. 8, 1903, Samuel Pierpont Langley, a leading government-funded scientist, launched with much fanfare his flying machine on the Potomac. It plummeted into the river. Nine days later, Orville and Wilbur Wright got the first plane off the ground.

Peter Cook   www.academy-of-rock.co.uk

Why did these bicycle mechanics succeed when a famous scientist failed? Because Langley hired experts to execute his theoretical concepts without going a series of trials and errors.

Studying the Wrights' diaries, you see that insight and execution are inextricably woven together. Over years, as they solved problems like wing shape and wing warping, they made several mistakes which inspired several adjustments all of which involved a small spark of insight that led to other insights. Their numerous mistakes led to unexpected alternatives, which, in turn, led to the numerous discoveries that made flight possible.

The discovery of the electromagnetic laws was also a 'failed' experiment by Oersted in 1820 which led to the derivation of Maxwell's Laws and which opened the doors to our modern age of electricity and electronics.

To find out more about such things read Michael's latest book "Creative Thinkering". For me, this relates to the comparison between the 'one-hit wonder' in music and those artists who learn from their early mistakes. For example, evergreen artists such as Pink Floyd, Madonna, Prince, The Rolling Stones, Radiohead and so on.

You have written some great books about techniques for divergent and convergent thinking. Could you say some more about this?

I don't use the terms divergent and convergent. To me thinking is either productive or reproductive. We are all born spontaneous and creative thinkers and then we go to school. In school we are taught what to think not how to think. It's as if we enter

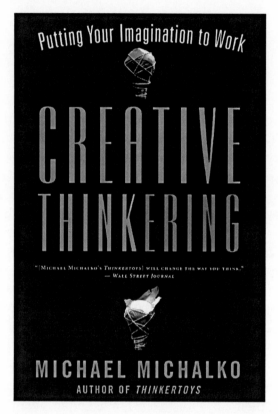

school as a question mark and graduate as a full stop. Typically, we are taught to think reproductively, that is on the basis of similar problems encountered in the past. When confronted with problems, we fixate on something we learned from the past that has worked before. We ask, "What have I been taught in life, education or work on how to solve the problem?" Then we analytically select the most promising approach based on past experiences, excluding all other approaches, and work within a clearly defined direction towards the solution of the problem.

Peter Cook   www.academy-of-rock.co.uk

Creative people think productively, not reproductively. Productive thinking is creative thinking. When confronted with a problem, they ask "How many different ways can I look at it?", "How can I rethink the way I see it?", and "How many different ways can I solve it?" Instead of "What have I been taught by someone else on how to solve this?" they tend to come up with many different responses, some of which are unconventional and possibly unique. With productive thinking, one generates as many alternative approaches as one can. You consider the least obvious as well as the most likely approaches. It is the willingness to explore all approaches that is important, even after one has found a promising one.

From talking to companies such as IDEO and from my own experience, there comes a point when some convergence is needed to successfully convert a creative idea into an innovation. I use the phrase "converge with care" as this is often done badly, so as to destroy the very novelty that you have tried to nurture. What views do you have on this?

This is where your intellect comes into play. In nature, it is the process of natural selection that converges the many into the few species that survive. Similarly, it is the intellect of the creative thinker that converges the many into one. Creative geniuses will then use their intellect to elaborate the idea by considering such things as substituting this for that or that for this, combining it with something else, adapting something to it, adding something, changing something, eliminating something, finding other uses, rearranging or reversing it in some way until their intellect is satisfied that this is the best way to converge the idea into an innovation.

It is the intellect that creates the convergence to successfully convert a creative idea into an innovation. Spencer Silver knew this when he invented a glue that did not stick. 15 years later we had the Post-it Note™.

Biology is a good teacher. Can you say more on this?

Creative genius operates according to laws of nature. Nature creates many possibilities through blind 'trial and error' and then lets the process of natural selection decide which species survive. In nature, 95% of new species fail and die within a short period of time. Genius is analogous to biological evolution in that it requires the unpredictable generation of a large quantity of alternatives and conjectures. From this quantity of alternatives and conjectures, the intellect retains the best ideas for further development and communication.

This is why the most distinguishing characteristic of genius is immense productivity. All geniuses produce. Bach wrote a cantata every week, even when he was sick or exhausted. Mozart produced more than six hundred pieces of music. Einstein is best known for his paper on relativity, but he published 248 other papers. Darwin, Edison, Rembrant were also very prolific. Shakespeare wrote 154 sonnets. Some were masterpieces, while others were no better than his contemporaries could have written, and some were simply bad. In fact, more bad poems were composed by the major poets than the minor poets. They composed more bad poems than minor poets simply because they produced more poetry.

Peter Cook   www.academy-of-rock.co.uk

Editor's note: Later on in this book we examine the continuously creative output of Bill Nelson, leader of Be-Bop Deluxe and Red Noise. Amidst a huge canon of work, Nelson consistently turns out some amazing gems. Prince adopts a similar approach, working tirelessly to in his search to find his musical destiny.

How then do we systematically introduce variation in our ideas? I loved Thinkertoys and undoubtedly there is a value in technique. What about the more general strategies for creating?

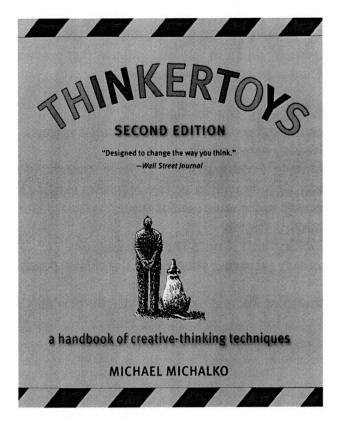

THINKERTOYS

SECOND EDITION

"Designed to change the way you think."
—*Wall Street Journal*

a handbook of creative-thinking techniques

MICHAEL MICHALKO

To produce variation in your ideas and for this variation to be truly effective, it must be 'blind.' In effect, you are emulating nature's genetic mutations. To count as 'blind,' the variations are shaped by random, chance, or unrelated factors.

Creative geniuses deliberately change the way they think by provoking different thinking patterns which incorporate random, chance and unrelated factors into their thinking process. This is why creative thinkers are able to look at the same information as everyone else and see something different.

The majority of my work in creative thinking is focused on the particular creative thinking strategies that creative geniuses used to provoke different thinking patterns that produced their original and novel ideas. They include:

- Making novel combinations
- Forcing connections between dissimilar subjects
- Thinking paradoxically
- Thinking homospatially - actively conceiving two or more discrete entities or two opposites existing simultaneously in the same mental space.
- Thinking visually
- Thinking metaphorically and analogically
- Actively preparing yourself for the chance discovery

These strategies liberate your creativity by breaking up your conventional thinking patterns and stimulating new thinking patterns by juxtaposing unlikely information.

What are the essential pre-conditions for creative thinking techniques to work?

Three important pre-conditions for creative thinking techniques to work are:

1.   Belief

The artist is not a special person, each one of us is a special kind of artist. Every one of us is born a creative, spontaneous thinker. The only difference between people who are creative and people who are not is a simple belief. Creative people believe they are creative. People who believe they are not creative, are not.

2.   Work at it

You must also have the passion and the determination to immerse yourself in the process of creating new and different ideas. Then you must have patience to persevere against all adversity. All creative geniuses work passionately hard and produce incredible numbers of ideas, most of which are bad. The more you practice creative, the more you lay down neurological patterns in your brain that are productive or reproductive.

3.   Apply your imagination

Lastly, you must put your imagination to work. Your brain is a dynamic system that evolves its patterns of activity rather than something that computes them like a computer. It thrives on the creative energy of feedback from experiences real or fictional. You can synthesise experience; literally create it in your own imagination. The human brain cannot tell the difference between an 'actual' experience and an experience imagined vividly and in detail. This discovery is what enabled Albert Einstein to create his 'thought experiments' that led to his revolutionary ideas about space and time. One day, for example, he imagined falling in love. Then he imagined meeting the woman he fell in love with two weeks after he fell in love.

I like Einstein's ability to think about relativity in space and love almost simultaneously! Are some company climates 'hard to crack' in terms of creativity? Do you have any success and war stories in this area?

Once a person has formed an image – that is, once he or she has developed a mind set or expectation concerning the subject being observed – these condition future perceptions of the subject. This principle helps explain why evolutionary change often goes unnoticed by corporate executives. The greater the commitment of the executive to their established view, the more difficult it is for the executive to do anything more than to continue repeating their established view. It also explains the phenomenon of a beginner who comes up with the breakthrough insight or idea that was overlooked by the corporations who worked on the same problem for years.

While most corporations strongly endorse a positive view of creativity, I've discovered that the same corporations routinely reject creative ideas. For example, at one time, the Swiss dominated the world watch industry. The Swiss themselves invented the electronic watch movement at their research institute in Neuchatel, Switzerland. It was rejected by every Swiss watch manufacturer. Based on their experiences with watches, they believed this couldn't possibly be the watch of the future. After all, it was battery powered, did not have bearings or a mainspring and almost no gears. Seiko executives, with no background in the watch industry, took one look at this invention that the Swiss manufacturers rejected at the World Watch Congress that year and took over the world watch market.

Apple Computer Inc. founder, Steve Jobs, attempted, without success, to get Atari and Hewlett-Packard interested in his and Steve Wozniak's personal computer. As Steve recounts, "So we went to Atari and said, 'Hey, we've got this amazing thing, even built with some of your parts, and what do you think about funding us? Or we'll give it to you. We just want to do it. Pay our salary; we'll come work for you". And their experts laughed and said, "No". So then we went to Hewlett-Packard, and they said, "Hey, we don't need you. Go back to school".

Here a few more examples:

- When Univac developed the computer, they refused to present it to the business world because they said it only had scientific applications.
- Pierrre Pachet, a renowned physiology professor and expert declared, "Louis Pasteur's theory of germs is ridiculous fiction".
- Fred Smith's Yale University management professor gave Fred a 'C' because Fred's paper proposal to provide over-

night delivery service was not a feasible business idea. Fred's proposal became Federal Express. Incidentally, every delivery expert in the U.S. doomed FedEx to failure as they said no one will pay a fancy price for speed and reliability.

- "The wireless music box has no imaginable commercial value. Who would pay for a message sent to nobody in particular?" said David Sarnoff's associates, in response to his urgings for investment in the radio in the 1920s.

Michael Michalko can be found at www.creativethinking.net

"Music ... can name the un-
nameable and communicate
the unknowable"

Leonard Bernstein

The Music of Business

We recently delivered one of our masterclasses on business excellence mixed with music for The BBC, Bloomberg TV and The Independent.

Whilst being interviewed the media asked if I was able to wrap up MBA level business lessons in one sentence using rock and pop songs. Something of a challenge, given that I spend some of my life teaching MBAs, where length and business jargon are generally considered to be more important

Anyway, I rose to the challenge, so here are 10 creative business/music tips, reduced to the bare minimum. A kind of 'Lean MBA' for busy people.

1. Bad Romance: Lady Gaga – If you're having trouble in a work relationship, change what you're doing, rather than banging your head against the same wall.
2. Reasons To Be Cheerful: Ian Dury – Reasons to be cheerful at work include: being listened to; doing things that count; understanding why they matter; being part of something; not having to do pointless tasks; getting meaningful feedback on what you do and so on.
3. Like a Virgin: Madonna – To succeed in business, treat each day like it's the first time.
4. Knowing Me Knowing You: Abba – If you want to serve someone really well, find out their wants, needs, whims, foibles, fancies, fantasies, fanaticisms and ensure what you are offering touches the parts that others cannot or dare not reach.

Peter Cook   www.academy-of-rock.co.uk

Madonna's influence lives on to this day

5. Who Killed Bambi?: The Sex Pistols – Separate conflict over work from conflict over personalities. You can have a good bun fight over a project, but once things are settled, move on and don't harbour grudges towards the people.

6. The Great Pretender: Queen – Leadership requires us to be a master of style. Dictator, sales person, facilitator, confidant, comedian, entertainer, counsellor. Know your own range.

7. I Can't Control Myself: The Troggs – Creativity without discipline rarely leads to innovation.

8. What Do I Get?: The Buzzcocks – Pay people well enough, but don't just focus on pay as the reward for work. This reinforces the conversation about 'What do I get?'

9. Walk On The Wild Side: Lou Reed – Encourage mavericks, madonnas and the odd primadonna at work if you want new things to happen.
10. Sexy MF: Prince – Style always wins over substance. Once you have got your product sorted, go for style every time.

"Anytime I have an idea, I'll make sure that I put it down so that when we do sit down to write an album, I don't have to dream it all out of thin air. I don't have to be creative on the spur of the moment, or spontaneously artistic. I just take advantage of whenever creativity strikes"

Neil Peart, Rush

Playgrounds of the mind: Scott McGill on improvisation and creativity

I was privileged to interview Scott McGill, a progressive rock and jazz-fusion guitarist. Scott has played with Percy Jones of Brand X and worked with Michael Manring, both well-respected fretless bass players. He divides his time between teaching, composing, performing and researching music, something of an idyllic lifestyle.

Tell me about your influences in terms of innovative music and improvisation?

I spent 10 years working with Dennis Sandole who was John Coltrane's teacher. It does not get much better than that. I've played with some of the best people on the planet in Casinos on the East Coast and Broadway etc. I also find that one of the best ways to extend yourself is to teach and research music. I've spent 20 years teaching, writing, playing freelance and improvising. That amounts to more than 10 000 hours of immersion in music.

**So you are the ultimate adaptive musician? Front of stage, in the studio, teaching others? I meet people who are good at one of these but rarely all three.
I'd guess that this requires some loss of ego and the ability to focus intensely on what you are doing at any one time?**

Peter Cook   www.academy-of-rock.co.uk

Yes. It's enthusiasm and focus really. I like learning and engaging deeply in many areas of music, which enables me to learn a great deal. The discipline of progressing in all of these areas is something I am interested in as it makes me feel as though I am working towards something meaningful. I also find that progression in one area usually facilitates progression in the others.

Take me back to the beginning

I started learning both reading and playing music. They were always married. I did not start out as many people do, by either learning formally and then starting to improvise 7 years later or vice versa. I began by picking up a few chords but very soon after took lessons from someone who did both reading and improvising. The ear is the instrument. Even if you are reading, you should always be able to hear it and vice versa. I learned music in a combined way from the inception.

Does formal learning have to drive out the possibility of improvising?

Not at all for me. The more I learn about theory, the better I get at improvising. I don't partition it. For me, rules are a release and not a barrier. That said, for some musicians, it is apparent that learning musical theory does hinder them from improvising and vice versa. I guess it's a question of mindset and it also depends on the training. Some of the best improvisers were formally trained, e.g. John Coltrane and Liszt.

www.academy-of-rock.co.uk   Peter Cook

When you are in the moment of creativity, what happens? What is teachable?

I lose all sense of time (not timing, ha, ha!). When I am creating I also become hyperfocused, like you can hear everything that is coming next and you have the ability to successfully predict what the other people in the band are about to do. I think that my senses are very acute in those moments. This is not really teachable. It has to be learned by experience. However, the vernacular – the notes, the chords are teachable. How sounds relate to one another. How things sound against one another. There's a lot of syntax and the ability to hear something new. My teaching is individualised and improvised and a lot rests on the student – which makes teaching music one of the hardest things to industrialise.

What about when people get stuck in improvisation? Are there things you do to help unblock them?

Listening to the same thing with fresh ears is one approach. Getting them to listen to new things is another. Sometimes changing the instrument or even the approach to the instrument is effective. For example by looking at the guitar up and down the neck instead of along the neck may make someone approach the instrument more like a piano or saxophone.

Here's a picture of one of Scott's famous fretless guitars:

Talking to Bernie Tormé and Bill Nelson over the years, I've been told that switching instruments is a great idea for creativity e.g. in Bernie's case to the

Sitar. Bill Nelson goes so far as to say that different guitars force a different attitude from the player. Incidentally, this is a great strategy for justifying multiple guitar purchases with your partner! Do you subscribe to the views about the instrument dictating the music?

www.academy-of-rock.co.uk   Peter Cook

Absolutely. The nuances of an instrument matter a great deal. I'd add the ideas of learning about concepts and then trying that out on an instrument. So theory for me is a practical tool.

What about the idea that the untrained ear is everything with respect to musical creativity?

An intuitive approach does not exclude formalism and I've known and worked with great players in both categories. The argument, "Don't read music or your creativity will be shut off" does not stand up to scrutiny. I can give you examples on each side of that argument in every case. I always wanted to read music so that I could grab some sheet music and use the notes in a different way.

So, you see a music score as a playground rather than a cage?

Precisely. I listen to a score and think, "What could I do with that?" For example, I'm doing a couple of pieces that have borrowed ideas from Ravel at the moment. This illustrates the skill of what Tom Peters called 'Creative Swiping'.

Tell me about the idea of anticipatory skills and how this relates to the idea of leaning into the future in business.

I'm reading a lot about anticipation at the moment – especially the work of K. Anders Ericsson. Ericsson discusses how the fastest and most accurate typists are the ones who can quickly anticipate the next move. His theory of Deliberate Practice has influenced me greatly.

Peter Cook   www.academy-of-rock.co.uk

Ericsson states that, "In sum, the superior speed of reactions by expert performers appears to depend primarily on cognitive representations mediating skilled anticipation rather than faster basic speed of their nervous system". This suggests that conceptual anticipation or 'seeing the next move' is a key transferable skill.

Where does innovation come from in music, given that we're all working with the same 12 intervals? – maybe more in your case as I know you specialise in playing fretless guitars?

I don't know really. From what I know there are many millions of combinations of the twelve pitches not to mention the inclusion of rhythm, form, timbre, tempo/time, etc. There are always microtones for those who want a different sound other than the twelve standard pitches as well. I do play fretless guitar and enjoy it thoroughly. I like the different vibrato and glissando possibilities and the fact that you can shape a note a bit more after striking it that you can with a fretted guitar. It is difficult to play in tune though.

Scott McGill may be contacted through his website www.scott-mcgill.com

Transferable lessons

1.   Use structures AND creativity to achieve mastery in any field.
2.   Use anticipatory approaches to stay ahead. This may involve deep listening to your own performance and that

of those around you, whether we are talking about music, business or other fields of endeavour.

3. Adopt an emotionally intelligent approach to working with others, sensing and responding to minimal signals to help change course along the way.

"One chord is fine. Two chords are pushing it. Three chords and you're into jazz"

Lou Reed

Two Pints of Lager and a Packet of Crisps, Please: Punk creativity

Creativity can be a deliberate process, assisted by techniques and explicit strategies which we work with, such as Superheroes, Six Thinking Hats, The Disney Creativity Strategy, Synectics and so on. In other cases it is a more accidental and intuitive process. Saccharin is a classic example of an innovation developed by accidental creativity, discovered when Constantin Fahlberg noticed a sweet taste on his hand one evening. He connected this with the compound that he had been working on in the laboratory.

This article concerns the accidental discovery of the top ten punk rock hit "Two Pints of Lager and a Packet of Crisps, Please" by Max Splodge, enthusiastic motorbiker and leader of the quintessentially English cult punk band Splodgenessabounds from Bromley in South East London. I've performed with Max and escorted him, Wilko Johnson and Norman Watt Roy of Ian Dury fame through French customs, after they had both had a 'heavy night' performing with John Otway, otherwise known as 'Rock'n'Roll's greatest failure' in France. In doing so, I extracted a number of stories of mayhem from the crazy world of Rock'n'Roll en route back to the UK. On the next page there's a picture of us consuming two pints of lager with a Blondie tributess, but no crisps.

Max conceived the title of this classic song whilst trying to procure said drinks and condiments at a local pub in South East London. Faced with a packed bar, Max kept urging the bar staff to serve the beer with his refrain "Two Pints of Lager and a

Packet of Crisps, Pleeeeze". Shortly after this experience, Max thought, "That's the title of a hit record". The rest is punk rock history. Splodgenessabounds went on to have several chart hits and it is unlikely they would have been so successful without the two pints of lager.

What are the business lessons here? Well, creativity and innovation involves seeing something different in the ordinary and converting that idea to a commercial success. Just as Percy Shaw, who invented cat's eyes, noticed something different in the ordinary, when he realised that he had been using the reflection of tram tracks to navigate in the dark.

Most other people in Max's situation would have just seen the desire to procure 1400 millilitres of lager and some munchies.

www.academy-of-rock.co.uk   Peter Cook

Splodge saw the potential for a top ten punk rock hit. There's a huge difference in the fortunes that come from noticing the difference. He also then went on to put the idea into action, which is perhaps even more important than having the idea.

At the same time great ideas can come out of rather small and seemingly unimportant observations, so its important to keep all your senses open. Having asked many people in the course of my seminars, there are also a number of common environments in which creativity flourishes. For example:

- Whilst driving.
- When travelling by train.
- Whilst listening to music.
- Doing the washing up.
- Having a shower.
- Drinking in a bar.

... and a whole series of other occasions when people are 'off task'. What works for you?

Naturally creative people tend not to use explicit creativity techniques, rather they use unconscious recipes that often mirror the tools and techniques used by people who prefer to have a set of 'rules for creativity'. In my experience, many rock stars prefer an intuitive approach over creativity toolboxes. Both approaches are valid. Take a look at the article from Michael Michalko and the book "Best Practice Creativity" to discover some of the main techniques that people use to replicate the habits of highly creative people.

Creativity lessons from Punk Rock:

Punk rock creativity lesson # 1. Spot sublime ideas in the mundane as well as the profane. Above all else tune in to the world around you.

Punk rock creativity lesson # 2. You don't need brainstorming if you have the creative muse.

Punk rock creativity lesson # 3. Ideas are nothing, execution is everything.

Punk Rock creativity lesson # 4. If you don't find creativity comes to you naturally, remember that there is a suite of creativity techniques that model the habits of naturally creative people.

"8:15 to 10, rock history. 10 to 11, rock appreciation in theory. And then band practice till the end of the day"

Jack Black on a Punk Rock curriculum for "The School of Rock"

Richard Laermer on Punk Marketing

Richard Laermer is a marketing genius from New York, who helps his clients break away from tried, tired and worn out marketing strategies and tactics. I met him when we were both delivering keynotes at International Marketing and Leadership conferences in Athens. Imagine our surprise and delight when we learned that we had both written books with Punk in the title: Richard's "Punk Marketing" and my "Punk Rock People Management", available free by e-mailing me. We became superfast friends and I wanted to find out more.

What is the essence of "Punk Marketing"? What marketing demons do you want to purge?

Punk Marketing started when my friend Mark and I were talking at a grungy bar sometime in the mid 2000s. We realised that many marketing people were entirely complacent. Punk rock arrived when the music industry was at its most complacent. The Osmonds, The Carpenters, Debbie Boone and so on. When Punk rock started, with The Clash, The Sex Pistols, they crashed that party, they screwed up the mentality of the music industry and they made them wake up. So we said, let's do the same thing for marketing now that punk rockers did for music in the 1970s.

What can marketers do that is genuinely innovative?

Marketers need to take more risks. They look at a marketing project and say, our customers are stupid so let's just put out a fun tagline and some cute colours and everybody will think we're great. It's all just clichés. What marketers should be saying is, "We suck. People don't love us for what we should be. We need to be much more crazy, using ideas that everyone laughs at, the one that disturbs our competitors, the one that makes shareholders and board members nervous, because that's the only thing that will give us any long term value".

What do you consider to be the future in social media? What should go into room 101?

I got a call from a major fast food chain whose ads were being mocked on YouTube. They wanted me to stop it happening and I said to the Marketing Director, "Are you crazy? People are taking time out of their day to make videos about your ad. You should be paying them!"

Peter Cook   www.academy-of-rock.co.uk

People have to realise that controlling the message is about NOT controlling the message. You must then participate in the conversation. That does not mean just letting people talk – it's like what Stalin said: You do have to control the people some of the time. That means participating in the arguments, telling people the rules of engagement, making sure that people see what you are all about etc.

Companies like Procter & Gamble can say a lot on social media but if it doesn't pass the shake and shiver test, it can go in room 101.

With the tendency to graze, the 'punk marketer's' job is to get them to stop for more than a millisecond?

You've gotta get people thinking. And I know that's hard. The consumer is not stupid. The consumer is constantly talking and getting information. To think that somehow we're gonna get their attention because we are more intelligent is ego. Kodak died because they thought they knew more than the consumer.

Peter Cook

They never stopped to think that we know more than an old complacent camera company from the suburbs. You have to look around, pick up the intelligence and learn from it. Get the info that you're scared to hear about.

Give me a couple of lessons from Punk Marketing

When you avoid risk, you die – When someone says to me, "This isn't the right time", I'm the first person to find their competitors doing something really great and sending it to the people who just told me it isn't the right time. General Mills and Kellogg Company found this out in the Great Depression of 1929. At that time Kellogg was the number one cereal maker. In the Depression Kellogg decided not to do any more advertising, due to the recession. They even cut their worker's hours to 30. But General Mills, then the number two, decided to go the whole hog, even introducing Betty Crocker in the biggest possible way. Guess what? General Mills became number one during those tumultuous years and still is. Kellogg learned a lesson I'm sure they never forgot.

Make enemies – These do not have to be the competition like Pepsi with their 'Beat Coke' ambition. It only has to be positioning yourself against an alternative. For example Oil of Olay made an enemy of a concept – they said that the enemy is aging. Women bought it (literally).

Give up control – Realise that the control is all in your head. Domino's Pizza used to have a terrible reputation, typified by the phrase 'Dominos Sucks'. They turned it round and told their customers, "Yep we suck so we've changed completely". They

Punk Marketing
and Punk HR

Creative
companions

London,
New York,
elsewhere

introduced new recipes. Within six months they had turned their reputation round.

Richard Laermer can be contacted at his website www.laermer.com and via Twitter and The Huffington Post.

"Everything I do is totally spontaneous"

Ritchie Blackmore

PART 3 – Innovation

Introduction to Part 3 – Innovation

Innovation is complex and rarely the preserve of the lone inventor or creative person these days. We often require people from different disciplines to come together around an innovative enterprise and this requires us to make diversity of thinking work to advantage.

We begin our journey of diverse viewpoints on innovation with Lady Gaga and Prince. In particular these artists have stood on the shoulders of giants and improved upon their strategies for success. This is as rare in the world of music as it is in the business world.

We take some timeless lessons from history via an examination of how the various protagonists managed to change the world view on the periodic table, which is a pivotal discovery with major impacts on modern scientific thinking. Innovators must be great persuaders and there is much to be learned from this story. This connects well with a piece I originally wrote for Sir Richard Branson on the internal barriers to innovation where we consider the issue of selling ideas and the impact of time and timing on the success ratio of ideas: innovations within companies.

Innovation at work requires a climate that supports it and several of the articles in this section point to this fact. Contrary to what most people believe, opulent organisation design does not always enhance innovation. We take some stark lessons from hard rocker Bernie Tormé, who has literally been there and done it with people like Ozzy Osbourne and Deep Purple's Ian Gillan. His examples taken from direct experience of working in Stax studios and other places where great records were made is instructive here. We also draw some parallel lessons about innovation climate and how to lead innovators from the examples of Canadian Punk Band Deerhoof and Andy Warhol and The Velvet Underground.

In some cases innovators are ahead of their audiences. Marc Bolan and Richard Strange, the godfather of punk are particularly good examples here. Richard Strange has had the privilege of working on Harry Potter, Batman and many more. He shares a number of insights on innovation and creativity from a diverse career as an entrepreneur across the arts. We'll be doing some joint events alongside the book going forward, combining lessons from business and the art world.

We look at design innovation via the example of Vigier guitars. Vigier have combined form and function in taking the guitar on a few steps from the dominant designs of Fender and Gibson. Design is vital in an age where copying products can be done rapidly.

We also take a look at the personal qualities of innovators such as Marc Bolan and Steve Jobs. Given the way that many recruitment companies and HR Departments operate these days, I have some doubts that Steve Jobs would have got a job in a company these days ...

"You have to be unique, and different, and shine in your own way"

Lady Gaga

Born This Way: Lady Gaga on innovation

Lady Gaga is a music and business phenomenon. Strategy, innovation marketing, finance, HR, operations, social media and so on, all rolled into one. Setting aside all the controversy over her music, fashion etc., what might an innovator learn from Lady Gaga about her approach to business? In case you have not caught up with Lady Gaga, take a look at her "Edge of Glory" video on YouTube, with lyrics dedicated to her grandfather: Here's five transferable business lessons that you can learn from Lady Gaga:

Lady Gaga's music is thrilling and based on some solid foundations. Her music springs from 80s and 90s electro pop and dance music, drawing upon a range of influences, such as Bowie, Queen, Elton John, Madonna, Britney Spears and Michael Jackson. Many people are creatures of habit in terms of their musical tastes – just think of classic rock bands like AC/DC, U2 and The Rolling Stones who have not altered their musical recipe that much. Building on some well-established musical scaffolding makes Lady Gaga's music a very acceptable diet for consumers, young and old.

Gaga innovation lesson # 1. Innovate within the familiar range of the customer's expectation for maximum early impact. Build on that for long-term sustainability.

www.academy-of-rock.co.uk   Peter Cook

If Lady Gaga's music is in the familiar range, the presentation certainly is not. Or is it? Sure, people are shocked to see Lady Gaga attacked during her performance and then die in a pool of fake blood. But, remember Alice Cooper's electric chair executions and Madonna's on stage sex scenes for "Like a Virgin" on her Blond Ambition tour? Perhaps the difference is that Lady Gaga has learned from all of these people and improved the packaging and presentation of the theatrical elements that accompany her music. Top business thinkers such as Tom Peters have written about becoming a learning organisation. Unlike some businesses, Lady Gaga has actually taken notice of Tom's wisdom. We shall see if she continues to learn over time as there is always the danger that complacency can creep in when you are at the top of your game. I recall discussing this very point with Pfizer when they were the number one pharmaceutical company in the world. It's one thing to reach number one in the charts, something quite different to remain there.

Gaga innovation lesson # 2. Stand on the shoulders of giants if you want to innovate. Be a genuine learning organisation if you want to stay in business long term.

Lady Gaga has succeeded in an age where society is questioning the profit imperative of corporations and celebrities. How has she done this? By cleverly combining the profit and purpose ambition as Daniel Pink, author of "A Whole New Mind" points out. Gaga combines exceedingly clever cross branding (music, fashion, headphones etc.) with a number of social and humanitarian causes such as the Haiti earthquake, the Japanese Tsunami and various AIDS/HIV causes. This has enabled her to withstand a number of public relations crises when others would have crumbled.

Gaga innovation lesson # 3. Combine your social responsibility agenda with your business plan in a seamless way. Execute your plans with meticulous detail.

Lady Gaga has a shrewd approach to partnerships – working with evergreen stars such as Madonna, Elton John, Tony Bennett and Cher. This gives her access to a much wider market for her music and legitimises her brand across generations.

Gaga innovation lesson # 4. Use partnerships and joint ventures to enlarge your market share in ways that benefit all the stakeholders. Choose your partners wisely and in ways that provide genuine win-win benefits.

Lady Gaga has captured the hearts, minds, souls and bank balances of several generations through the clever use of social media, in ways that major corporations can only dream of. She has given her fans control of social media such as Twitter, Facebook, YouTube and so on. They have a shared identity and Gaga has allowed her fanbase to operate a 'market pull' approach to affiliation instead of using traditional 'push' approaches to marketing. If Gaga were writing a business book, she would probably have knocked Seth Godin, Paul Sloane et al. off the top of the Amazon charts on the business concept of 'crowdsourcing'. Gaga has captured an online army of advisers, salespeople and so on. Here's an example of her Twitter feed:

Lady Gaga @ladygaga   14h
Its the anniversary of BAD ROMANCE so were bringing back the hair tonight!!! #hotlikemexico littlemonsters.com/post/508b394ab…
Expand

Lady Gaga @ladygaga   14h
Check out this exclusive post on #littlemonsters littlemonsters.com/post/508b394ab…
Expand

Gaga innovation lesson # 5. Understand that social media is social and the powerful imperative of the word YOU in social media. People like social media to interact with their own lives and values.

The **Gaga** of **Business**

Innovate within the familiar range of the customer's expectation for maximum early impact. Build on that for long-term sustainability.

Stand on the shoulders of giants if you want to innovate. Be a genuine learning organisation if you want to stay in business long term.

Combine your social responsibility agenda with your business plan in a seamless way. Execute your plans with meticulous detail.

Use partnerships and joint ventures to enlarge your market share in ways that benefit all the stakeholders. Choose your partners wisely to provide genuine win-win benefits.

Understand that social media is social and the powerful imperative of the word YOU in social media.

Peter Cook   www.academy-of-rock.co.uk

"Too much freedom can lead
to the soul's decay"

Prince

Purple Rain: Prince on innovation

The name Prince is synonymous with innovation in music. From classy pop classics such as "Purple Rain", "Diamonds and Pearls" and "U Got The Look" through to high-class jazz, soul and funk, such as "Sign O' The Times", "Avalanche" and "We Live 2 Get Funky", working with artists such as Miles Davis, Chaka Khan, Stevie Wonder, George Clinton and so on. Check out some of Prince's performances on YouTube to see what I mean.

> *"Doing a residency in any particular city requires a large repertoire to ensure repeat business".*
> Prince

Unlike many performers in rock's monarchy, a Prince live performance is often different every night. This is because Prince operates from a menu of 300 songs, which the band may be called upon to play at any time. Many other artists prefer to perfect and then repeat their set night after night, because it is seen as a huge risk to make mistakes in front of a stadium size audience. What are the parallel lessons for businesses that are interested in being fast, nimble and continuously innovative? Here are some:

Prince innovation lesson # 1. If you want to be nimble and adaptive, practice, practice, practice.

To reach mastery in improvisation paradoxically requires intensive detailed preparation. What looks like a seamless performance is the result of many hours of preparation and Prince is meticulous in this respect. I had the chance to study this at close range at one of his concerts at London's Roundhouse recently. Watching Prince perform is better than attending a masterclass on the everyday habits of a polymath in action. With a wink of his "3rd eye" Prince simultaneously:

- Sends signals to the sound crew that his guitar sound needs adjustment.
- Requests the lighting crew to make changes to the lighting.
- Gestures to the band to extend/shorten/vary the songs using a series of hand signals whilst simultaneously dancing.
- Works the audience through various facial expressions, winking at an audience member within the middle of pulling a contorted guitarists' ecstasy pose whilst playing a solo etc. Prince plays with the irony of the whole rock performance genre in ways that make you forget he is 56 years old.
- Operates his array of floor pedals with his feet, fixes microphones and so on.

It's all going on with Prince – every muscle, limb and corpuscle are centred on his performance and more importantly the performances of those around him and the expectations of his diverse audiences. It's no surprise that he is adored by musicians who understand that to get better you need to surround yourself with people who are better than yourself. It's also no surprise that lesser mortals loathe his unique combination of musicology and showmanship as it's just 'too good' in comparison to their own skills.

We have discussed the idea of mastery in previous chapters under the heading of the '10,000 hours effect', popularised by Tom Peters and, more recently, Malcolm Gladwell. The idea of prepared spontaneity contradicts what some so-called creativity and innovation gurus say on the subject, yet we constantly see parallels across many industries. Sloppy creativity produces sloppy results in many businesses as well as in the rock business. We saw an example of this in the "Spinal Tap" article with John Otway's World Tour, which failed due to too much creativity and not enough meticulous execution of the ideas. In contrast, Prince is a master of detail, having delivered 21 nights in succession, plus different aftershows every night all night long.

Prince innovation lesson # 2. Be a boundary crosser if you want to create a sustainable advantage in your marketplace.

Prince is also a master of fusing musical genres and influences outside his core style to innovate. This enables him to still exert a major influence on artists of the 21st Century, such as Lady Gaga, Beyoncé and many others. In business, the ability to cross mental boundaries is the parallel skill set, exemplified by companies such as 3M and Google.

Google in particular is a great example of a large enterprise that encourages experimentation and practice. In a recent interview Google's CEO said:

> *"One of the primary goals I have is to get Google to be a big company that has the nimbleness and soul and passion and speed of a start-up."*

This means that, unlike most large companies, Google must tolerate and embrace failure if it is to continue to innovate. Practice makes perfect but it also allows for mistakes. Google's approach may mean that we will see driverless cars in the future, powered by Google's developments in geolocation.

Prince innovation lesson # 3. Innovation = Perspiration + Inspiration. Be prepared to sweat it out as well as glow with your ideas.

Prince's level of risk taking on stage is perhaps greater than other artists such as Celine Dion, who aims for a perfect, polished performance, which can be reproduced night after night.

When Celine Dion showcases the individual band members in what appears to be a loose jam, the order and sequence of each individual solo is preset in advance. In contrast, Prince will call out individual band members for a solo on the fly.

"I used to be more involved with every aspect of everything onstage. I'm way more relaxed now. It feels like anything can happen".
Prince

This requires every band member to be watching and waiting for the instructions that Prince gives to the band members. Both approaches rest on meticulous preparation and practice if you want to reach out for excellence. An object lesson for all – if you want to be a star, know that perspiration is much more important than inspiration.

The Prince of Innovation

If you want to be nimble and adaptive, practice, practice, practice.

Be a boundary crosser if you want to create a sustainable advantage in your marketplace.

Innovation = Perspiration + Inspiration. Be prepared to sweat it out as well as glow with your ideas.

Peter Cook   www.academy-of-rock.co.uk

"Mindless habitual behaviour is
the enemy of innovation"

Rosabeth Moss Kanter

Something In The Air: Developing an innovation climate

This article looks at the impact of the built environment and creativity, via a conversation I had with Bernie Tormé, guitarist for Ozzy Osbourne, GMT, Dee Snider and Ian Gillan.

**Monster of Rock
Bernie Tormé**

Before we begin, here's the science bit. Leading academics such as Gareth Morgan, Jane Henry and others talk about the impact of 'climate' on creativity and innovation. But, what is meant by climate? For me it is the psychological and physical environment. There are no standards as to what works in either area, merely empiricism. For example, some people need quiet reflective space to create, others need close friends, others the comfort of strangers and so on. In his research on climate Swedish Professor, Goran Ekvall, studied what went on in a Swedish newspaper office. He discovered that the team working on the women's pages was always winning prizes whilst the newsroom never did. On further analysis, the biggest difference between the teams was in their sense of humour. Enjoyment does not appear as a line on the company balance sheet, but clearly this intangible asset makes a critical difference in this and many other examples.

If the impact of the psychological environment on creativity and innovation is hard to pin down, then so is the impact of the physical (built) environment. The common assumptions is that more opulence = more creativity and innovation and very large corporate campus style environments are built on such assumptions. Yet the reverse is also true in business and music. Starting with music, the history of Rock'n'Roll is littered with examples of brilliance emerging from rather shabby recording environments. Bernie gives us a bird's eye tour:

"When I visited Sun studios in Memphis I was astonished. It's just a shop basically, that produced some of the greatest sounding and culture changing records ever made. The same is true of Chess in Chicago, Stax, Motown in Detroit, scruffy shopfloors. I would also have said the same about Kingsway (earlier called the original De Lane Lea) where House of the Rising Sun was recorded, and virtually all of Hendrix's early output up to Wind Cries Mary. All the Gillan stuff and lots more. It was a complete claustrophobic dump. And IBC in Portland Place where all of the early Who stuff

was recorded. All of those places sounded wonderful with a decent engineer. And as for Regent Sound, where all those initial Stones hits were made, an absolutely horrific place."

Bernie's experience is not confined to Rock'n'Roll. Christof Zürn at www.musicthinking.com describes Richard Wagner was something of an innovator in terms of his goal to 'think as a musician and act as a designer and entrepreneur'. He used his many skills without compromise against all odds like a 19th century Steve Jobs. Wagner designed the interior of his music hall in Bayreuth with the focus on acoustics above comfort: the simple chairs are made from wood (fabrics would absorb the sound), the musicians are hidden in a deep orchestra pit so the audience would not be distracted, there is no heating and no climate control. So, no compromises or comfort for the performers then! I then asked Bernie what happened later on.

"I remember lots of grandiosely stunning studios from the 80s. The ones in the 70s were far more workmanlike, like garages. Funny what happened in the 80s. Part of a bubble I suppose, like all the other bubbles. It was more about attracting 'clients' with the bells and whistles rather than a decent sounding room and an engineer who knew how to use it. Hence all those electronica records.

I must admit to never liking places like The Townhouse etc. I did a bit there and lots in the old Marquee studios, lots of glass, marble, stone and polished steel. Both looked great and sounded like complete shit. I am ranting ...."

Ranting aside, I think Bernie has spotted a very transferable point here, that having it all does not necessarily lead to great results. Sometimes desperate conditions produce excellence. A lot of the world's breakthrough drugs were developed in shabby laboratories by hard-pressed scientists, starved of resources and so on.

It's well worth watching the movie "Muscle Shoals" to deepen your insight into the impact of the physical and psychological environment on high performance. The studio Muscle Shoals produced greats such as Aretha Franklin, The Rolling Stones, Alicia Keys, Etta James, Percy Sledge et al.

My personal experience of a great climate was in leading innovative science teams for The Wellcome Foundation. Wellcome was run as a not for profit charity – perhaps the only 'Bruce Wayne styled' philanthropic pharmaceutical company. Wellcome was badly managed but well led. Let me explain:

Wellcome was badly managed in what some modern HR professionals would now expect: people were more or less allowed to get on with their work; we worked in a Portakabin for much of the time although there was investment in the equipment we needed to do the work; conflict was considered OK; Team building was done in the pub; Performance appraisals were limited, Performance Related Pay non-existent and so on.

However, Wellcome was extremely well led: Leaders let people get on with things, expecting that they would want to do their best; failure was tolerated provided that people learned from mistakes and so on. This meant it did not need the complex control systems and bureaucracy beloved of modern HR departments. Wellcome produced four Nobel Prize winners in its time. Many modern pharmaceutical companies with slick HR departments, beautiful buildings, performance related pay systems and so on would kill their grandmothers just to win one.

The Wellcome example is mirrored by some of the classic Quaker inspired companies such as Cadbury, Pilkington and Johnson and Johnson. When HR managers tell me that pay is the only determinant of high performance, I think they have fundamentally missed the point that engagement and commitment starts at the recruitment stage of the process. Time after time we see that great leaders invest considerable time in the attraction process rather than trying to apply "sticking plasters" to disengaged employees.

There is no doubt in Bernie's, and my mind, that a healthy psychological and physical environment makes a huge difference to peak performance at work. However, opulent physical surroundings do not always make for greatness, neither do 'cuddly HR practices'. That said, there's no need to

The Business School Run by Rock Stars
22 Jun 2012
What can the likes of Madonna or Prince teach people about running a business? London consultancy Human Dynamics believe leadership and communication skills can be taught through rock music.

1:39

Bloomberg

Peter Cook   www.academy-of-rock.co.uk

throw televisions out of hotel windows or set light to guitars as we have done on a couple of occasions at corporate events.

Bernie and I offer in-depth masterclasses on the creative process and how that translates into innovation. Events are punctuated by live demonstrations from a master of squeezing musical creativity out of thin air. Usually without spontaneous combustion of guitars, unless absolutely required! You can check these out on Bloomberg TV, BBC TV and BBC Radio 4 via the Academy of Rock Website.

"An important scientific innovation rarely makes its way by gradually winning over and converting its opponents. What does happen is that the opponents gradually die out"

Max Plank

The Music of Chemistry

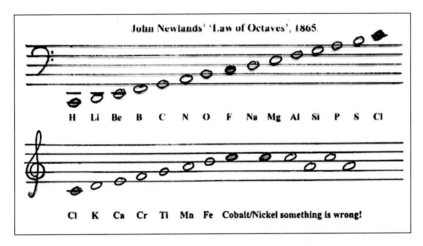

Three fascinations have filled my life: Science, Business and Music. Creativity is the art and discipline of noticing connections between things and this prompted me to write an article about the connections between music, chemistry and innovation.

It was Döbereiner that first noticed the idea of patterns of the elements and, in 1828, he proposed the notion that the elements could be classified into triads, based on their properties. It took 30 more years for French geologist de Chancourtois' to develop the idea. de Chancourtois' organised the elements by their atomic weights and published his work in 1863. It's most interesting to note that his ideas were largely ignored by the scientific community as he used geological terms to describe his insight.

Business operates in several "foreign languages" such as finance, marketing, operations, computing, HR and so on. To be an effective influencer, it is wise to be as fluent in these as possible if you are to successfully persuade others about the value of your ideas.

Lesson for Innovators: Work in the language of your target audience!

In 1865, John Newland came up with his theory of octaves for the elements, organising the elements into groups of 8 and using music as a means of explaining his theories to the Chemical Society in 1866, who refused to publish his work, suggesting that it was frivolous.

There is a time to be serious and analytical with your presentations and another time to be lighter. Admittedly the concept he was trying to convey was complex and therefore the use of a metaphor was helpful to get the message across, but clearly his audience did not feel it was backed with sufficient gravitas to be taken seriously.

Lesson for Innovators: Persist with your metaphors!

There were some flaws in Newland's theory as some elements did not quite 'fit' the law of octaves. It took a few more years before Mendeleev produced the essential breakthrough of what we now consider the basis of the modern periodic table. So confident was Mendeleev of his theory that he left spaces in the table for elements that had yet to be invented.

There are inevitably questions asked of new ideas and by leaving spaces in his table Mendeleev will have addressed questions

Reihen	Gruppe I. R^2O	Gruppe II. RO	Gruppe III. R^2O^3	Gruppe IV. RH^4 RO^2	Gruppe V. RH^3 R^2O^5	Gruppe VI. RH^2 RO^3	Gruppe VII. RH R^2O^7	Gruppe VIII. RO^4
1	H=1							
2	Li=7	Be=9,4	B=11	C=12	N=14	O=16	F=19	
3	Na=23	Mg=24	Al=27,3	Si=28	P=31	S=32	Cl=35,5	
4	K=39	Ca=40	—=44	Ti=48	V=51	Cr=52	Mn=55	Fe=56, Co=59, Ni=59, Cu=63.
5	(Cu=63)	Zn=65	—=68	—=72	As=75	Se=78	Br=80	
6	Rb=85	Sr=87	?Yt=88	Zr=90	Nb=94	Mo=96	—=100	Ru=104, Rh=104, Pd=106, Ag=108.
7	(Ag=108)	Cd=112	In=113	Sn=118	Sb=122	Te=125	J=127	
8	Cs=133	Ba=137	?Di=138	?Ce=140	—	—	—	— — —
9	(—)	—	—	—	—	—	—	
10	—	—	?Er=178	?La=180	Ta=182	W=184	—	Os=195, Ir=197, Pt=198, Au=199.
11	(Au=199)	Hg=200	Tl=204	Pb=207	Bi=208	—	—	
12	—	—	—	Th=231	—	U=240	—	— — —

about the level of scientific knowledge present at that time. In doing so, he increased the credibility of his concept since he demonstrated that he did not have all the answers. Successful influencers are often honest about weaknesses in their arguments contrary to what some people believe.

Lesson for Innovators: Ensure your theories explain gaps in current knowledge!

These stories illustrate the powerful forces that can operate to prevent a new idea or concept from coming into being. It points to the need for inventors and innovators to understand and navigate such barriers if breakthrough ideas are to come into being. They are also great examples of pattern spotting as a creative act. We explore barriers to intrapreneurship later on in this book.

www.academy-of-rock.co.uk   Peter Cook

"Innovation has nothing to do with how many R & D dollars you have. When Apple came up with the Mac, IBM was spending at least 100 times more on R & D. It's not about money. It's about the people you have, how you're led, and how much you get it"

Steve Jobs

Innovators: Marc Bolan

I met Lesley Ann-Jones recently, Freddie Mercury and Marc Bolan's biographer. This caused me to write some personal reflections on Marc Bolan, who influenced my life and music hugely. Bolan arrived on the music scene for me at the impressionable age of 14. In the midst of Slade, Bowie, Mud, Alice Cooper et al, he stood out as being a very gentle soul, although Lesley tells me that he was a very determined character, having once knocked on the door of Simon Napier-Bell and said he was going to be a big star, which got him started on the road to his first big hit. In case you are not so familiar with Bolan's beginnings, some background is useful.

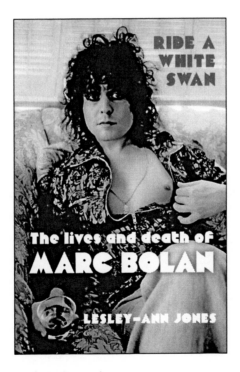

Peter Cook

Marc Bolan was turned on to music by Rock'n'Roll, especially Gene Vincent, Eddie Cochran and Chuck Berry. In the early 1960s Bolan became a Mod and then a Hippy, perhaps a series of odd transitions. Bolan subsequently moved to Paris, where he allegedly lived with a wizard. Later on, John Peel took an interest in Marc's first underground success – Tyrannosaurus Rex. The transformation came when Bolan went electric and he shortened the name to T. Rex. Bolan is considered to be one of the founders of glam rock. He married poetry with catchy rock guitar hooks that were developed from his Rock'n'Roll influences. His record sales accounted for approximately 6% of all sales in the UK market at the height of his success. But what was he like as a person?

Single-mindedness and mindfulness

For someone with a big ego, Bolan was generous of spirit, collaborating with David Bowie, Jeff Lynne, Elton John and many others. He also had an obsessive, relentless streak in him yet everybody he dealt with loved him. He even turned his back on the mighty John Peel, who felt that Bolan had sold out when he went electric in order to win fame. This is single-mindedness indeed, but Bolan was very progressive about his music, wanting to move on from the hippy sound that Tyrannosaurus Rex represented. This offers us an object lesson in personal reinvention. Sometimes you leave people behind when you change what you do.

A rare breed

In psychometric type terms, Marc Bolan is thought to share my own Myers Briggs type of ENTP. Might that explain why I was so drawn to him? ENTPs are reckoned to account for about 2.5% of the population (a rare breed as there are 16 types which would make the average around 6%), ENTPs are described as clever, usually verbally as well as cerebrally quick, with a love of argument. They tend to have a perverse sense of humour and tend towards innovative approaches. ENTPs do not suffer fools gladly. In general, however, they are genial, even charming, when not being harassed by life. This seems to describe Bolan to a tee. It seems that these qualities were accompanied by sheer drive and a desire to achieve.

Bolan was someone who was not trapped by the past, although there are echoes of Rock'n'Roll his heroes in his music. Bolan even recorded Eddie Cochran's "Summertime Blues" as one of his favourites. If you are musically inclined take a listen to 50s rockers such as Cochran and compare them with some of T. Rex's greatest hits. I'm sure you will hear some parallels, done in a most flattering way.

What, then can we take away from Marc Bolan's example?

- Be focused, but gracious to those around you at the same time.
- If you want to innovate in a discipline, respect the past but do not become trapped by it.
- Play is essential if you are to be creative.
- If you change what you do, be prepared to lose some of your followers.

"If you want something new,
you have to stop doing
something old"

Peter Drucker

Strategies for innovation in music

In this article Ben Weinlick of Canadian Innovation and Creativity Consultancy The Think Jar Collective interviews Deerhoof, who are quoted by The New York Times as "one of the most original rock bands to have come along in the last decade". Ben interviewed one of Deerhoof's founders Greg Saunier.

Ben Weinlick: I'm interested in hearing a bit about the creative process of how you guys make your albums. Is it true that you guys don't really record in a formal studio but wherever you find a bit of space?

Greg Saunier: Well, I'm not going to say we never have recorded in proper studio, but we almost never do. We record in various homes using a basic home recording setup. The four members of the band don't live in the same city anymore, which tends to make this a necessity.

Ben Weinlick: Do you find that this style of "nomadic" album recording helps with your song writing and creativity?

Greg Saunier: When you're forced to work around constraints, then you have to look for other tools to use. Like for me not being able to set up drums in a New York apartment because it will drive the neighbours nuts, I have to use electronic drums to record. One time late last spring we were doing a college show that was meant to be outside, and then this horrible rain storm came. On a moment's notice they moved us for awhile into this blank empty room where the only thing in it was a piano. While all the guys had to tear down the PA system outside and bring it in, I went over to the piano and decided it was a great opportunity to record some piano for a couple songs on the album. I brought out the laptop, put it on top of the piano, used the built in laptop microphone and recorded into Garage Band. As a result, there's a ton a piano on the new record. So, sometimes those difficulties end up getting you fired up.

Ben Weinlick: Tell me something of how you learned to play.

I think I got my idea of how to play rock'n'roll music from hearing the Rolling Stones when I was a little kid. It was a big turning point for me. There's a kind of looseness to the way that they play together, and an unpredictability to each individual person's part. Like when Keith Richards plays one of his riffs, one time he'll start it on beat 1, and the next time on the and-of-1, and the next time on the and-of-4, or maybe leave it out completely. You don't know what's coming and then that causes a ripple effect within the band. I love the sense of carefree pleasure that comes across from the Rolling Stones. It's like they know that it's ragged, unpredictable, bold, brash, and they don't care. It's like they enjoy the tension that's created between a group of people that all have different personalities and trying to work it out with each other and never quite get it. Whatever kind of mystery was created in their sound, is one I feel like I'm still trying to solve decades later.

With Deerhoof, when we play it's similar. When the magic is really happening and I feel like, "This is how we're supposed to play together!", it's when everybody is contributing some unpredictable element; everyone is throwing in surprises that we never rehearsed. That's when we're figuring "it" out. Of course you never reach the point when you really figure it out. There's a zone where everything is just slightly beyond your ability, a little bit harder than what you can actually do. Think about the Olympics recently; athletes talk about that all the time. The "zone" is the place where you're reaching for something that's just a little bit more than what you can do, and that's where it feels the most creative.

Ben Weinlick: This reminds me of Mihaly Csikszentmihalyi. He spent 40 years researching creativity and coined the term flow, which basically you just described and defined. Flow is where your abilities are pushed just to the point where it's a little bit beyond you and brings you to that "in the moment" sort of thing.

Editor's note: We discussed the idea of flow in Part 2 of this book.

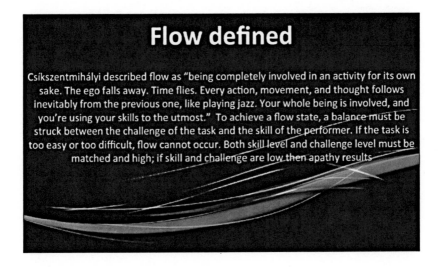

Flow defined

Csíkszentmihályi described flow as "being completely involved in an activity for its own sake. The ego falls away. Time flies. Every action, movement, and thought follows inevitably from the previous one, like playing jazz. Your whole being is involved, and you're using your skills to the utmost." To achieve a flow state, a balance must be struck between the challenge of the task and the skill of the performer. If the task is too easy or too difficult, flow cannot occur. Both skill level and challenge level must be matched and high; if skill and challenge are low then apathy results

Greg Saunier: It's like being in a room full of people and going and tapping someone on the shoulder and you haven't planned out what you're going to say. It just forces you into this situation where you have to come up with something.

Ben Weinlick: You mentioned tricking yourself into creativity earlier. Can you share what some of those tricks might be?

Greg Saunier: Oh totally. I have to kind of rotate the tricks. There isn't just one trick that you can absolutely count on.

1. Sleepiness – Sleep deprivation happens to me a lot when we have to fly somewhere on tour that is really far away. Like when we go to Europe, you get there when you think it's time to go to bed, but it's 10 in the morning. When there is that lack of sleep, and just as you're about to fall asleep there is the unconscious desperately trying to assert itself, I hear music in my mind and it seems to be more original than normal.

Editor's note: This has been noticed in many domains and we are beginning to understand more about the processes associated with the state of drowsiness through neuroscience. Certainly this experience is not unusual.

2. iTunes randomness – I'll just go on the iTunes music store and listen to previews of like, completely random stuff that I've never heard. Even if I do that for like half an hour, it's such an easy way to hear totally unfamiliar music and then afterwards my mind is filled with a bunch

of vague musical sounds that are all jumbled together. Then for a time, they get mixed up in a fun way and I start to hear new musical ideas in my head that really aren't any one particular song I heard.

Editor's note: Random provocation is mentioned as a creativity technique in the chapter on Oblique Strategies. Other techniques that build on this principle include "Forced Relationships", "Morphological Analysis" and "The Catalogue Method".

3. Role play – Sometimes I also try to picture one of my favorite musicians, especially if they haven't done anything really good for a while. I'll imagine what I wished they'd do. I'll imagine what I wished their next album sounded like. Projection can be a great creative trick. You pretend you're such and such guitar player, or singer.

Editor's note: The notion of projection and fantasy is a well-known creative technique which is embodied in techniques such as "Superheroes" and "Wishful Thinking".

You can find Ben Weinlick and The Think Jar Collective at www.thinkjarcollective.com

Richard Strange: The godfather of punk on creativity and innovation

What's the link between Harry Potter, Jarvis Cocker, Twiggy, Led Zeppelin and Robin Hood? Richard Strange of course! Quoted by Johnny Rotten on the BBC's 'Punk Britannia' as the man who invented punk, author, academic, Robin Hood's executioner and the man who ate Harry Potter...

Richard Strange is 'punk rock's illegitimate godfather', having preceded The Sex Pistols, The Damned, The Ramones and The Clash with his highly influential pop art band 'The Doctors of Madness'. Richard's career has spanned pop art, punk, writing and acting, most famously for his film roles in Batman, alongside Jack Nicholson, in Robin Hood and Harry Potter plus a number of other film noir masterpieces. I interviewed Richard close to where I first encountered The Doctors of Madness at London's Marquee club.

Strange views on personal creativity

Peter: What gets you in the creativity zone when you are composing?

Richard: I always was and still remain a word junkie – I love a good lyric. I love a good text or a good idea that is eloquently expressed. And rather tragically I wasn't into Rock'n'Roll. I loved writers like William Burroughs, Jack Kerouac, the Beat Generation at the age of 13-14. I also set my standards quite high. I have tended to think, if I've heard that rhyme before I'm not gonna use it unless I absolutely have to. If something sounds like a cliché it probably is. So I'm very meticulous in staying away from the obvious rhyme – the obvious sequential lyrical development I'm very aware that use words that many people wouldn't touch with a bargepole.

Peter: There is a large body of research starting with Wallas (1926) which suggests that creativity relies on a lot of unconscious work, spread out over time, rather than the instant flash of inspiration. The artist Jean Cocteau and the mathematician Henri Poincaré concur. Just witness these quotes:

"The role of this unconscious work in mathematical invention appears to me uncontestable, and traces of it would be found in other cases where it is less evident. Often when one works at a hard question, nothing good is accomplished at the first attack. Then one takes a rest, longer or shorter, and sits down anew to the work. During the first half hour, as before, nothing is found, and then all of a sudden the decisive idea presents itself to the mind.... it is probable that

this rest has been filled out with unconscious work". Henri Poincaré – Mathematical Creation

"Often the public forms an ideas of inspiration that is quite false, almost a religious notion. Alas! I do not believe that inspiration falls from heaven. I think it rather the result of a profound indolence and of our incapacity to put to work certain forces in ourselves. These unknown forces work deep within us, with the aid of the elements of daily life, its scenes and passions, and, when they burden us and oblige us to conquer the kind of somnolence in which we indulge ourselves like invalids who try to prolong dream and dread resuming contact with reality, in short when the work that makes itself in us and in spite of us demands to be born, we can believe that this work comes to us from beyond and is offered us by the gods. The artist is more slumberous in order that he shall not work. By a thousand ruses, he prevents his nocturnal work from coming to the light of day". Jean Cocteau – The process of inspiration

So, does your creativity come out in bursts or do you develop things over time as per the examples of Cocteau and Poincaré?

Richard: Words and songs don't pour out of me. They are hard wrought. For example, I was asked recently to write a piece for the closing credits of a Hollywood film, Dark Hearts, which was a real thrill. They asked me to write song for the closing credits and it was a case of writing something that portrayed the themes but not the narrative.

It had to deal with the themes of betrayal, addiction, dependency and so on and these were my way into writing the song. The last scene is in the desert with the protagonist screaming at the heavens. I know as an artist that certain sounds will work and others won't. It had to come in with a vocal on the 1st bar and so on. So I spent two days trying the first two lines out, working out whether it was in 4/4 or 3/4 and just searching for the right sounds and words. My poor kids must have been driven crazy listening to me trying all this out.

Peter: So, you use the concept of 'immersion' as a method for creating? What about the idea of detachment, being 'disconnected' from the topic, rather like an arts director seeing their work from a dispassionate viewpoint.

Richard: Absolutely, I like to become absorbed in a piece. I find recording to be a wonderful tool for writing. Sometimes words feel good, but they don't sound good. And sometimes the reverse is true. Recording and playing back gives a great sound picture and the sound of words, in songwriting as in poetry, enhances and emphasises the meaning. On detachment, that depends on the song. Some songs are observational, some are immersed in the moment and the emotion. Different songs require the writer to adopt a different viewpoint.

Peter: Tell me some more about how you manage to compose something different without falling into the trap of 'karaoke Rock'n'Roll'? After all there are only so many combinations of music out there and we are bombarded by the stuff. In other words, how do you stay fresh?

Richard: I only ever write a song if I believe it MUST be written. If it brings something new to the table. If it doesn't already exist 'out there'. I keep notebooks to help with song creation – a trait shared by Bill Nelson. I always have done. Hundreds of them! I jot down a phrase, a word, a rhyme, a thought. Something I hear on the radio - a misheard conversation on a bus. Then I sift, refine, edit, try out conflicting ideas to see if sparks fly

Peter: Some people swear by techniques to help them innovate, such as using random stimuli or reversal. Others use a more intuitive approach. Are you aware of any particular personal techniques or rituals that you find helpful to escape mainline thinking?

Richard: Burroughs always recommended the cut-up method to escape writers block. But he also held that by setting the word free of the confines of syntax and obvious context, you liberated the 'true' meaning. Word falling... image falling... etc. It's a useful tool, but not one that I use as a staple of my process.

Musically, it's good to write on an unfamiliar instrument. To get an unfamiliar approach. The hands too easily form the shape of a familiar chord for me if I pick up a guitar, and I fall into cliché progressions. But if I sit down with an accordion, say, there is NO familiarity whatsoever.

Strange views on managing creatives

Peter: I know you have a rather amusing story about Richard Branson and the music industry. Can you tell me more?

Richard: I had came up with the idea of 'Cabaret Futura', a mixed media club with performance artists, poetry, short films and so on. We'd get people like Depeche Mode, Soft Cell, The Human League, Echo and the Bunnymen, Spandau Ballet, Richard Jobson and so on. Richard Branson became very interested in signing me to Virgin. We arrived on Richard's boat in Little Venice with a copy of my album "The Phenomenal Rise of Richard Strange" on cassette. He loved the first track and made me an initial offer of £54 000 for the album. I declined. He loved track 2 and came back with £58 000. Track three did not go down so well and he dropped the offer to £42 000. I thought he would like the final track and the offer went back to £54 000 – I thought I'd better accept at this point!

They were also signing bands like Simple Minds The Human League, Japan, Culture Club, Heaven 17 – bands that were much easier to market with good haircuts. The Phenomenal Rise referenced Edith Piaf, Berthold Brecht, Jacques Brel, electric disco and so on – much more difficult to market.

Overall, I'd say that record companies did not, and do not, offer much help to artists who wanted to break away from accepted music paradigms. Added to that I was always able to assist in my own inimitable way ha, ha! For example, I opened the Manchester Virgin Megastore launch event on my back in a comatose position and ended up in a worse state. Record companies don't always understand such things!

Peter: Can pop innovate given the huge changes in the way we use music these days?

Richard: There's never only one strand in popular culture or society. There's always at least two and they usually go in opposite directions. For example, when I think about how we listen to music these days, one of the trends is to listen to it with 255 000 people in a field called Glastonbury, another one is to put two headphones in your ears and listen to it completely one your own. These two phenomena are both happening at exactly the same time in history, in terms of how we enjoy music and how music is delivered to us.

The old model of the music business is in its death throes. What's replacing it, this monster called 'new media', has an appetite for music that's like nothing we've ever had before. It doesn't matter if it's a telephone, a computer, a website. It humanises the inhuman. Everyone wants music. But they want it in different places and for different reasons to what they used to use it. It's also more transient and disposable.

Peter: What should the record industry do now? Is it the engine room of its own innovation or destruction?

Richard: The idea of the pop star as we understood it, like the Stones, David Bowie and Madonna is over. Rock music is now just a series of reprised poses and posturing. It is impossible to hold a guitar without referencing Jimi Hendrix, Pete Townsend or Keith Richard. It really has all been done. And that's tragic for our kids. What chance do they have except as purveyors of pastiche?

Peter: Music now can be considered to be the mixing of genres. In some cases what emerges is sublime. In other cases, something else comes out. How do you see the thin slicing of genres, which is probably a marketing invention.

Strange and wonderful

www.richardstrange.com

Peter Cook

Richard: Music is all recombinant DNA. It is just banging two existing rocks together and seeing what spark is produced. I think musical genres are a total marketing invention. All music is mongrel. The Beatles rehashed a bit of Country and Western, a bit of old Rock'n'Roll and a bit of Tamla Motown and came up with Merseybeat. The Stones did the blues – Sonny Boy Williamson, John Lee Hooker, Chuck Berry. What were Oasis except the Sex Beatles? – a bit of attitude from here, a bit of melody etc. What was Paul Weller ever apart from an accretion of influences? David Bowie was Lou Reed, Scott Walker, Anthony Newley, Iggy Pop, Jacques Brel and Lindsay Kemp. But the SUM of those parts, those existing elements, was something we would call 'original'.

Richard Strange's website is at www.richardstrange.com

"Music is the wine that fills the cup of silence"

Robert Fripp

Andy Warhol and the Innovation Factory

Andy Warhol, The Factory and The Velvet Underground were synonymous with a groundbreaking synesthesia in music and art in the 1960s. Their influence has been pervasive over nearly 50 years on people such as The Sex Pistols, The Doctors of Madness, The Cure, The Psychedelic Furs, Patti Smith, Vaclav Havel and many others. Simply stated:

> *"The first Velvet Underground album only sold 10 000 copies, but everyone who bought it formed a band".*

Here we're looking at the qualities that led to the success of The Factory as a music innovation incubator, with parallel lessons for businesses wishing to make innovation part of their 'business as usual' activity. I noticed over many years of teaching

Peter Cook   www.academy-of-rock.co.uk

MBA programmes in creativity and innovation that these link exceptionally well with the four 'P's of innovation. I've linked the four 'P's to songs from the great retrospective album by Lou Reed and John Cale "Songs for Drella" – Drella being an allusion to Andy Warhol – a combination of Cinderella and Dracula. Get yourself a copy of this superb album and have a listen while you read this piece. It brings the topic to life in ways that reading does not achieve.

1. Person – This refers to the creative leader and their relationships with those they lead. Above all else, the creative leader is able to get people who would not choose to work together to do great things together. In terms of Andy Warhol's factory and Cale and Reed's album, the first song "Open House" makes reference to the grating tension between the Factory's personalities. In particular, Reed and Cale were unlikely collaborators. It was Warhol's role as an enabler and, as some would say, a master manipulator, that made things happen.

2. Place – Place refers to both the physical (built) and psychological environment. Clearly The Factory was a colourful environment in pure physical terms, but a fun space is never enough to make new things happen on its own. Companies such as Oticon, Semco, Innocent Drinks and Google are experts in creating environments that encourage new thinking. See also the article 'Something In The Air' for more on this.

The Factory could be seen as a business incubator or 'hothouse' in modern parlance, with Warhol demonstrating lots of permission giving behaviours and creating a micro-climate where different things could happen. John Cale said:

> "It wasn't called The Factory for nothing. It was where the assembly line for the silkscreens happened. While one person was making a silkscreen, somebody else would be filming a screen test. Every day something new".

Check out "The Trouble With The Classicists" on the "Songs For Drella" album, listening carefully to the words, to understand this point more clearly.

3.   Product – Innovative products are ones, which genuinely fulfill a want or need in a sustainable and different way. Classic examples of innovative products include the Post-it Note™, Pilkington glass, the Dyson vacuum cleaner, which allegedly had 5127 prototypes, the Polaroid camera, telephone and Kentucky Fried Chicken, which was another product borne out of persistence.

Innovative products bring together disparate wants or needs e.g. an iPhone brings together personal organisation, photography, music, e-mail, horoscopes … Oh yes, and it can be used as a phone! The sustainability point is important since this separates a 'fad' from the 'future'. Check out the article on the guitar to read about the Fender Stratocaster. What 'product' did The Factory produce though? Uncompromising real life 'art' that dealt with subjects hitherto untouched by the art world – at the same time Warhol's protégés produced an unending supply of pop art such as the images of Marilyn Monroe and Campbell's Soup. Or, was the product simply a mind shift as to what constituted art? Clearly Warhol continues to exert an influence on the direction of art some 45 years later. Lou Reed and John Cale epitomised aspects of The Factory's art production line in the words to the dissonant viola piece "Images".

4. Process – Most successful innovative enterprises have either understood or explicit processes for converting bright ideas to sustainable and profitable innovations. Andy Warhol was a workaholic, contradicting the view that creativity was about waiting for inspiration to arrive. He favoured perspiration above inspiration and this is neatly summarised in Cale and Reed's words to their song "Work".

Andy Warhol clearly understood what business schools would call 'innovation climate', building a physical and psychological environment where people would be inspired to think great ideas and then convert them to finished product. We've looked at these principles and precepts in the article on The Beatles and they are summed up in the rich picture overleaf.

Provocative Questions

Here are some questions to provoke your own innovation factory listed under the 4 Ps:

1. Person – Have you got the right people in the right balance to make innovation regular and frequent? Inventors, Innovators and Entrepreneurs?
2. Place – Have you got a physical and psychological environment that encourages creativity and calculated risk taking?
3. Product – Do you seek constant innovation in the products and services that you provide?

4. Process – Have you got reliable processes for divergent thinking (creativity), convergent thinking (deciding) and converting decisions into profitable innovation (implementation)?

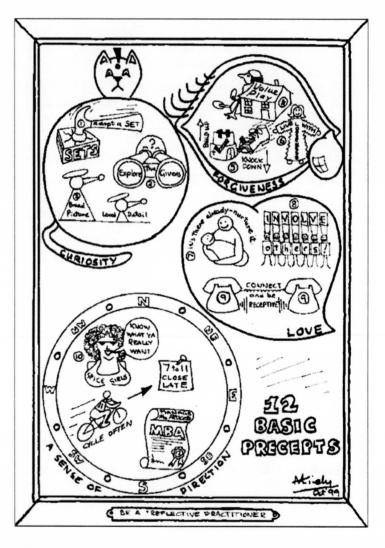

"Being good in business is the most fascinating kind of art. Making money is art and working is art and good business is the best art"

Andy Warhol

Breaking barriers to intrapreneurship

Virgin is a prime example of a company that would not have been able to develop into 200 discrete business without encouraging a number of intrapreneurs or what I like to call 'firestarters' within it's ranks. Intrapreneurs are responsible for innovating inside a company, sometimes with the luxury of greater levels of funding than they may be able to access as an entrepreneur, yet not always with the same freedoms afforded them as entrepreneurs, depending on the company culture. The internal entrepreneur must therefore be skilled in the art and discipline of navigating barriers to the conversion of an idea to a sustainable innovation. What then are the typical barriers to getting your idea off the ground inside a company?

Selling your idea

Novel concepts are by their nature fragile and must be communicated clearly and potently to those who must sponsor them. If your concept is complex, it's of vital importance that you communicate the concept simply to those who will advance funds, people and time to develop the idea. We frequently see how complex concepts fail in the Dragon's Den. Of course Dragon's Den is not real life and you are normally given more time to pitch your idea at work, nonetheless simplicity, brevity and potency are key to capturing the interest of your sponsors. Try the seven words test: Can you explain the raw essence of your idea in seven words or less? If you can do that, then getting 5 minutes to explain your idea, it's unique qualities and long term benefits is going to be much easier.

Peter Cook   www.academy-of-rock.co.uk

Never give up

Spence Silver took 15 years to convince 3M that his idea for "a glue that wouldn't stick" was a winner (the 3M Post-It Note™). Ken Kutaragi nearly lost his job at Sony Corporation when he worked for Nintendo in his spare time developing what became the Sony PlayStation. Kutaragi found a product champion in the form of Norio Ohga, Sony's CEO, who recognised his creativity, when most of the senior management team saw his project as a distraction rather than a serious piece of new product development. By 1998, the PlayStation provided 40% of Sony's profits. The lesson here is to play the long game. Overnight successes as an intrapreneur are the exception, not the rule.

However the type of persistence we are talking about here is not the "If at first you don't succeed, try try again" type. I call this headbanging aka "doing the same thing over and over, expecting a different result". I prefer this maxim "If at first you don't succeed, try something different" – this is a kind of flexible persistence, which requires emotional resilience (the ability to recover rapidly from life's setbacks, learn from it and move on – what I call The Chumbawamba effect). We'll explore this later on in the book.

Tight fit or misfit?

By their very nature, novel ideas often appear to be outside the scope of the current business strategy, unless you have a leader like Sir Richard Branson who encourages a more divergent approach to intrapreneurship. Most new product and service innovation succeeds because the product or service augments or is consonant in some way with existing approaches. So, you can increase the probability of adoption of your idea by demonstrating how it fits in. When Akio Morita introduced the Sony Walkman, he considered the lifestyle compatibility issue by making shirts with a pocket designed to hold the device, thus solving the problem of "where to put it?". Always think about the way in which your idea will be used and ensure that it fits in with the social and technical systems, which will improve adoption.

Time and Timing

Timing in the innovation game is everything. Da Vinci 'invented' the Helicopter several centuries too late! Had Clive Sinclair introduced his C5 20 – 30 years later when concern about the environment had turned into activism, he might have been more successful. I used to work for Sir Trevor Jones at The Wellcome Foundation, a philanthropic pharmaceutical company which was devoted to innovation. He had a "too difficult" in-tray, for ideas that people had submitted that could not be implemented due to various issues including timing. He systematically recycled the items in the "too difficult" pile so that they could be launched when timing favoured their introduction as an intrapreneur.

The other vital issue is securing sufficient time to work on your idea to convert it to an innovation. Pharmaceutical company Roche take the view that intrapreneurs must be allowed time to innovate and have applied the '20% bootlegging principle', originally developed by serial innovators 3M and also adopted by Google. Basically, this allows intrapreneurs to spend 20% of their time on non-job related speculative projects. Intrapreneurship has delivered Gmail and Google News amongst other innovations within Google.

You are not an island

Sir Richard Branson may live on Necker Island, but he gets out all over the world to look for ideas and intrapreneurs. In the same way, it's no good behaving like you are an island as an intrapreneur. You need to diffuse and spread your ideas widely in the company to build up support. Get out and talk to people who can help you spread your idea. Many companies

use innovation champions to support intrapreneurs. A champion will help you diffuse your idea within the company and may help you when the night is darkest. Virgin Atlantic's herringbone-designed private sleeper suites were the result of the championing of the work of young designer Joe Ferry. Richard Branson said that Joe's work put us years ahead of the pack and made for millions of very happy horizontal fliers.

Internal Combustion

To sum up it is worth reminding ourselves of Clark's Law of Revolutionary Ideas in terms of becoming a 'firestarter'.

Every new idea, be it in science, politics, art or any other field, evokes three stages of reaction:

> *"It's impossible. Don't waste my time"*
> *"It's possible, but it's not worth doing"*
> *"I said it was a good idea all along"*

The intrapreneur successfully manages these barriers to convert a promising idea into a sustainable innovation.

"It is in Toyota's DNA that mistakes made once will not be repeated"

Akio Toyoda

Design innovation: The guitar

I attended a guitar master class with Christophe Godin and was struck by the quality of the Vigier Guitars he used in the master class. Since I spend a lot of my time consulting with companies looking to innovate and the world of guitars is confounded by 'dominant designs' from the usual suspects, I decided to interview Christophe to find out what is unique and different about Vigier Guitars. Before we start, we review what the business academics say about new product innovation.

Successful design is a perfect union of form and function or style and substance. Good functionality contributes to style rather than being included for its own sake. The Fender Stratocaster is a good example of this, where the curvaceous body design is both attractive and provides stability in the guitar. For more than 50 years, the Stratocaster has remained a dominant design in many respects, due to the initial form and function elements that Leo Fender introduced, largely on an intuitive basis.

Most successful innovations accidentally or otherwise conform to a number of criteria identified by Isenberg:

Relative advantage – They offer superior benefits or sometimes a combination of benefits previously unavailable. Sometimes a number of secondary gains accrue through the use of the innovation?

Compatibility – The innovation fits in with current thinking or practice. It is packaged so that it is easily accepted. It's often easy to spot examples where things don't fit in with society and so on.

Complexity – Successful innovations are often easy and quick to understand by others. Simplicity is especially important when trying to diffuse new ideas into a crowded and busy marketplace.

Trialability – New things often need to be tried out before people can commit. This is especially true for innovations that are radical departures from what currently exists.

Observability – Innovation must be made visible? This is especially important for services, which are largely invisible to consumers. For example, it's not possible to see high speed broadband WiFi but you know whether you are able to connect to the Internet quickly.

How then do Vigier guitars stand up to more than 50 years of market domination by Gibson and Fender? I asked Christophe.

Peter: Given that the guitar has not managed to 'escape' from dominant designs popularised by Fender et al, what innovations have Vigier been able to bring, both in form and function?

Christophe: Vigier guitars are lighter due to the fact that there is 10% of graphite in the guitar neck to keep it away from twisting. Even after hours of playing it standing, I feel no pain or stress holding it.

Certain features are also very innovative, such as the tremolo system, which is attached via needle bearings. This means no friction and a very smooth action, which makes an impact on my playing. The guitars are very versatile and allow me to play stuff, which would require playing three different guitars in one song.

Peter: According to George W. Bush, there is no French word for entrepreneur! Consequentially, France would not be at the top of my list of guitar manufacturers in the world:-) Can you tell me something of the history of Vigier and how they have innovated from a fairly stagnant marketplace for guitars?

Christophe: Ha, ha! I'd say Patrice Vigier had a very clear vision about what he wanted to achieve from the very first day he started to build up his very first guitar. The search of perfection has always driven him, and he has always been very interested in innovation. He was the first to incorporate carbon into his guitars and everyone called him crazy. Patrice is NOT

THE WONDERFUL CHRISTOPHE GODIN

and he kept on sticking up to his idea. The results have proved him right.

Peter: There do seem to be quite a groundswell of people choosing Vigier guitars. I know Dave Sturt, who plays for Steve Hillage, Gong and Bill Nelson. Also Scott McGill, the jazz-fusion guitarist. Who else is playing Vigier instruments?

Christophe: Ooooh the list goes on forever. Actually, Ron Thal (Guns and Roses), Shawn Lane, Roger Glover, Geezer Butler, etc...

Coming back to where we started, the transferable points re innovation and Vigier guitars are:

- An obsessive pursuit of the marriage of form and function in the design process. Nothing is wasted.
- An application of many of Isenberg's points re successful innovation, especially the points about relative advantage and compatibility. This is of particular value in markets where there are already existing products and services in existence.
- An unwillingness to be constrained by the 'dominant design' of the Fender Stratocaster. 'Escapology' is often more hard in an established market and it takes great courage and the ability to see beyond limitations created by a strong brand.

Look at more of Christophe's superb playing and incredible sense of humour at www.christophegodin.com For more on Vigier check out www.vigierguitars.com

"If something is easy to repair,
it is easy to construct"

Leo Fender on reverse
engineering

Innovators: Steve Jobs

Richard Bandler, the godfather of NLP, reminded me whilst I was writing this article, of how death is life's ultimate change agent, in terms of its ability to make way for the new. Watch Steve Jobs Stanford University talk on YouTube re this point, shortly after he contracted cancer. It is a breathtaking speech.

Steve Jobs was a remarkable if abrasive man, so, when he died, I pondered what he leaves us as a lasting legacy:

As Apple's maxim is "Think Different", Jobs took a different view on a number of things. He was no friend of market research, preferring intuition as a spur to innovation. It's a characteristic he shares with Leo Fender, who was not a great guitar player, but designed intuitively great features into his ground-

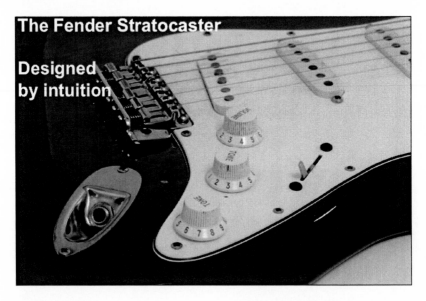

The Fender Stratocaster

Designed by intuition

breaking Fender Stratocaster guitar.

Jobs' 2nd legacy was his insistence that technology needed to fuse style and substance. This was modelled down to the last detail in Apple's products, which made them functionally superior as well as design icons.

People's love of the Apple brand was evident in their tributes to Jobs. I believe this arises not just out of style for its own sake, but because Jobs fused style with substance.

Steve Jobs was what the academics would have called a deviant innovator. Chances are that he might not have got through an HR interview in a corporate company, as a scruffy young man who spent too much time investigating things outside the scope of your business and buying equipment without seeking permission.

www.academy-of-rock.co.uk   **Peter Cook**

If Jobs managed to slip through the recruitment net, it's likely that HR would have fired him as a troublemaker. Professor Michael Kirton would describe Jobs as an innovator in terms of his innovation style – see the article on Hendrix and Clapton for more on this. Innovators tend to have the following qualities:

- Do things differently rather than incremental development.
- Can be abrasive. Jobs was renowned for this.
- Are unconstrained by the past in the way they think.
- Act on intuition rather than being addicted to data.
- Take larger risks than adaptors.

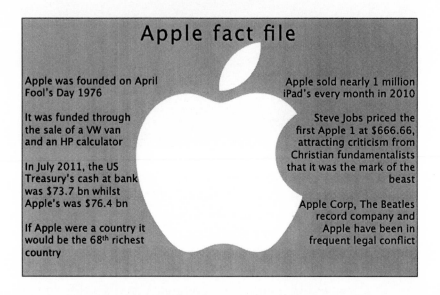

Apple fact file

Apple was founded on April Fool's Day 1976

It was funded through the sale of a VW van and an HP calculator

In July 2011, the US Treasury's cash at bank was $73.7 bn whilst Apple's was $76.4 bn

If Apple were a country it would be the 68th richest country

Apple sold nearly 1 million iPad's every month in 2010

Steve Jobs priced the first Apple 1 at $666.66, attracting criticism from Christian fundamentalists that it was the mark of the beast

Apple Corp, The Beatles record company and Apple have been in frequent legal conflict

If you want your company to innovate, HR departments and business leaders must at least tolerate and at best encourage people like Steve Jobs.

Peter Cook   www.academy-of-rock.co.uk

Jobs' 3rd legacy is his mantra, "Stay hungry, stay foolish". Comfort does not make for great innovation, nor does taking yourself too seriously. All too often hunger, naïvety and playfulness are driven out of corporate life with disastrous consequences for long-term innovation.

The credit crunch and the recession have exacerbated this tendency with people taking less and less risk in corporate life. Steve Jobs' last reported yearly salary was $1.

www.academy-of-rock.co.uk   Peter Cook

Steve Jobs' Innovation lesson # 1. Think differently if you want to innovate.

Steve Jobs' Innovation lesson # 2. Think across disciplines if you want to innovate.

Steve Jobs' Innovation lesson # 3. Stay hungry, stay foolish if you want to innovate.

"Innovation almost always is not successful the first time out. You try something and it doesn't work and it takes confidence to say we haven't failed yet … Ultimately you become commercially successful"

Clayton Christiansen

PART 4 – Leadership

Introduction to Part 4 – Leadership

Leadership excellence requires a mastery of ones own values, both in terms of maintaining stability and encouraging change. Leaders are responsible for introducing change, whether this is stepwise incremental change or a total reinvention. In the western world, this crucially means taking people with you rather than attempting to impose your will on others. Leaders must master the arts and disciplines of collaboration, improvisation and engagement if their visions are to take hold in the long term.

We start with a lighthearted reinterpretation of Britney Spears' song "Oops I Did It Again", reset in the context of learning companies. Change requires learning, both at superficial and more fundamental levels. Professor Adrian Furnham goes on to discuss a wide range of considerations for creative leadership and change, coming from an extensive track record in research and looking at what marks the sheep out from the goats in this area.

We take an unusual look at organisation structure via the medium of orchestras, jazz and rock music, concluding that, for the most part, orchestral and jazz leadership approaches are out and rock is in. The rock approach offers there is balance between structure and unfettered improvisation. Rock groups are also characterised by distributed leadership rather than centralised approaches.

A poorly studied area of leadership is that of followership. Several people who write on leadership through the medium like to suggest the notion of the leader as a rock star. We destroy

www.academy-of-rock.co.uk   Peter Cook

the myth in the chapter "Leaders need followers not fans". This is followed by an exemplar of humility in leadership through the example of Nigel Kennedy.

We indulge in a bit of personal leadership development via articles on stopping out of date behaviour at work and emotional resilience. The STOP button is the most valuable asset a leader has in helping an enterprise turn a difficult corner. Stopping bad things happening is much more difficult than starting new things.

We finish with four exemplars of bold reinvention with transferable lessons for businesses. Madonna and David Bowie are expert chameleons: changing; taking their existing audiences with them and; gaining new ones at the same time.

I had the good fortune to be asked to provide some coaching to assist Meatloaf's long-term singing partner Patti Russo in her personal reinvention. This provided me with a unique opportunity to learn from someone who has worked with some of music's greatest stars with some of the biggest egos on the planet.

We also examine the example of Bill Nelson, who took a principled decision to reinvent himself without concern for maintaining his audience. His principles for reinvention offer a fascinating insight into the mind of an authentic artist, untrammeled by the need to satisfy record company executives' sales targets.

Finally we have a little bit of fun with a spoof article on Bruno Mars. If you are not having fun as a leader, I'd question whether you are leading to the best of your abilities.

Peter Cook   www.academy-of-rock.co.uk

"I think life is far too short to concentrate on your past. I'd rather look into the future"

Lou Reed

Oops I Did It Again: Britney Spears on learning companies

A learning company is a company that learns faster than its competitors and agilty and speed of new product/service delivery is vital in today's business world. Many leading business academics, such as Chris Argyris, Peter Senge and Tom Peters have commented on this idea, which Britney Spears unwittingly stumbled upon in her classic hit "Oops, I did it again", I say in a deep sense of serious irony ...

In the context of business, I've taken "Oops I did it again" to refer to the tendency of businesses to repeat themselves, sometimes in the face of compelling evidence telling them to change course. Organisational learning can mean two things:

Single loop learning

Single loop learning involves improvement where we keep existing values and introduce new behaviours – this is often dubbed 'continuous improvement', where we look for better ways to do existing things. A number of business disciplines currently in vogue, such as 'Right First Time', 'Lean Thinking' and 'Six Sigma' have elements of single loop learning as an underpinning conceptual idea.

Even some older ones, such as 'Total Quality Management' and 'Continuous Improvement' are based on the same notion of single loop learning. This enabled Japan to revolutionise its industrial strength after the Second World War, following the doctrines of Dr J Edwards Deming. Single loop learning is the mainstay of much life in companies and it is necessary but never sufficient. What more do we need then?

Double loop learning

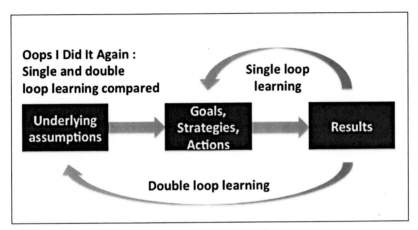

Oops I Did It Again : Single and double loop learning compared

This is a fundamental reassessment of the way we operate. What John Lennon would have called "Starting Over". Most organisations are complex adaptive systems and therefore have legacy systems and ways of working that need to be unwound if fundamental change is to take place. Double loop learning is often more radical and therefore, as a consequence, even more difficult. If, however, a business is in need of renewal, it is even more important that double loop learning should take place.

In general, companies find it intensely difficult to institute learning at an organisation-wide level, be it single or double loop learning. Marks and Spencer nearly went out of business through having such a strong culture that it did not learn from its customers. Manifestations of this included:

- Marks and Spencer's refusal to accept credit card payments other than their own store card for many years. They assumed their brand was bigger than their customers. The customers disagreed.
- A dogged insistence on only using British clothing manufacturers. Whilst it's possible to see this as having good ethics, it significantly increased their cost base, which made them very unattractive to consumers.
- Clothing designs that were considered 'dowdy' and out of touch. Somehow they lost touch with the zeitgeist.
- A disastrous initial expansion into Europe built on the belief that British products and values would be fully transferable to a European context. The market disagreed.

On the other hand, Toyota has based much of its growth in recent years on behaving as an organisation that learns, alongside other approaches such as lean thinking. This has given Toyota an incredible edge compared with their competitors. This is visible in one of the largest product ranges in the car market.

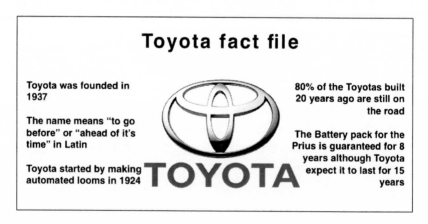

Toyota fact file

Toyota was founded in 1937

The name means "to go before" or "ahead of it's time" in Latin

Toyota started by making automated looms in 1924

80% of the Toyotas built 20 years ago are still on the road

The Battery pack for the Prius is guaranteed for 8 years although Toyota expect it to last for 15 years

Toyota have also pioneered the idea of 'mass customisation', where the end user gets to decide the specific features they wish to have in their car. We have also discussed this idea in the article on The Kaiser Chiefs.

Toyota Innovation

Leadership lesson from Britney # 1. Don't repeat yourself. Learn and adapt.

Leadership lesson from Britney # 2. If fundamental change is required, don't paper over the cracks with single loop learning.

Leadership lesson from Britney # 3. Customers switch brands rapidly these days. Keep them interested by not offering them repeat performances, especially when your market is agile and disloyal.

www.academy-of-rock.co.uk   Peter Cook

"My model for business is the Beatles. They were four guys who kept each other's negative tendencies in check. They balanced each other and the total was greater than the sum parts. And that's how I see business. Great things in business are never done by one person, they are done by a team of people"

Steve Jobs

Professor Adrian Furnham on creative leadership

Professor Adrian Furnham leads the way with his forthright views on business psychology, backed with a meticulous accuracy in the analysis that supports his provocations, compared with the usual suspects in this area. A rare breed: master academic, raconteur, prolific author and columnist.

I asked Adrian to give me a rapid tour of the creative dimension of leadership. For much much more on this and other topics, read his extensive repertoire of books, currently standing at sixty seven in number via www.adrianfurnham.com

www.academy-of-rock.co.uk   Peter Cook

Innovation in leadership

Peter: Please characterise the sorts of companies that are good at innovation. What about size? Does that matter?

Adrian: Companies that are good at innovation are often startups involving young people, technology, IT. They are often staffed by clever/imaginative people who see work as play rather than just to make money.

Generally speaking, as they get larger they lose this capability. It's also about the type of organisation. For example, you are not going to find these things in your local council. They are not selected for it and they are not rewarded for it. If anything, they are punished for it. If you are in sales and marketing organisation, they are up for creative ideas. If you are in pharmaceuticals, they are creative but it's much slower, deliberate and cautious.

The Japanese have this concept of Kaizen, which involves making, continuous, small improvements etc. The issue is about someone who does the job coming up with a better way of doing things. It's not some manager sitting in an office. It's the person doing the job. People should be rewarded for coming up with little ways to make things better. This also means that you should be allowed to fail. What we know about successful entrepreneurs is that they've all gone bankrupt at least once. If you want to get an innovative culture you need to put up with failure because you will start something and it will go badly wrong.

Peter Cook   www.academy-of-rock.co.uk

Peter: Coming back to the size issue, can elephants learn to dance? In other words, can larger enterprises organise things such that they remain nimble and responsive to their customers and markets?

Adrian: Yes they can but it takes effort. It may take the dynamism of a person like Steve Jobs. Jobs was clearly not an easy person to work with but he was a determined one who knew that, in his world, the only way to thrive and survive is to innovate all the time and have very high standards. Young elephants learn better than old ones; and they dance better if there is both joy in the activity and a nice reward for doing so!

Do leaders need to be emotionally intelligent?

Adrian: Let me give you an example that is both. The whole thing about emotional intelligence really took off – it is now manifest in the word engagement. We used to talk about job satisfaction, then job involvement, then commitment, now we use the word engagement.

We all want engaged staff, because they don't have to be managed so well, because the joy is in the activity. What puzzles me is the following. The emotional intelligence movement says that the emotionally intelligent manager is a better manager – they are able to understand and engage their staff better. However, the research says that the people who get on in business are able to 'kick ass'. What that means that rather than being empathic, they are in some senses the opposite. What they are

	Perception	**Behaviour**
ME	Self awareness	Self management
YOU	Social awareness	Relationship management

Knowing me, Knowing you
Emotional intelligence unplugged

able to do is to confront poor performance and there is nothing worse than having a manager who lets everyone off the hook.

I've done a study on this. Do you want your boss to be High on IQ, Low on EQ or High on EQ and Low on IQ? In other words, do you want them to be smartish and warm or clever, tough and cold? Well, if you ask men, they say bright, tough and cold. If you ask women they are a bit divided about this. The problem comes when an organisation needs tough decisions to be taken and sometimes people with high EQ fail to address the bottom line, in other words the Darwinian nature of the whole thing.

Peter: One problem with EQ is that you can be surrounded by feedback and fail to take the organisation forward?

Adrian: The 360 movement is famous for giving people multi-source feedback but it is only useful if you know what to do with it. Having an insight into what others think about you can be worthless if you don't know what to do to improve, change or develop.

Making innovation more frequent and probable

Peter: If innovation cannot come down to a simple cause and effect approach, what can leaders do that will make innovation more frequent and more probable?

Adrian: I'd say three things. One of the issues around innovation for leaders is the question of integrity. Nearly all leaders say they want creativity and innovation and then they punish it. Some don't want it at all, they want to be in control. So, if you want innovation, you have to put up with ideas that will not work. The Hawthorne experiment in the 1930s was a good example of this. Whilst you cannot risk the enterprise, you can risk a part of it and be known for open-ness to experimentation and risk taking.

Next, I do think that youth is attractive – Young people are less risk averse, have less to lose and to have a youth mentality is a good approach. I was with an organisation where the average age of the board was 63 – this is not good. So, look for and hire people that are imaginative and curious. But expect that some things will not work; and some ideas are simply wacky.

The alternative is to come in as number two. Some organisations are rather good at watching carefully what their competitors do and as soon as they have a success formula, they follow fast and learn quickly. Words like the agile or learning organisation. Now the bigger or older the organisation, the more difficult this is to do.

The language of creativity-cultivating workshops is particularly interesting. There seem to be five related models:

The muesli model – People need to unblock their creativity. They are in some curious way constipated and unable to let go and express themselves. In this sense creativity courses may be seen as laxatives.

The dominatrix model – Here we are told to unleash our creativity. Somehow one has been bound up, tied down, physically constrained from that most natural and normal of tasks namely being creative. So courses are liberators.

The arsonist model – Creative consultants and trainers aim to spark ideas and light fires. They see people as dry tinder just waiting for the right moment. Their job is to find ways of facilitating fire-setting ideas.

The kindergarten model – The problem appears to be that we have all forgotten how to be playful. Playfulness is apparently not only a lot of fun but it is also very productive. So our trainer helps us regress to a time when we were happy and quite unabashed to draw pictures, sing songs, etc.

The gaol-liberator model – The problem, you see, is that we have all been boxed in a sort of cognitive gaol that has stopped us... wait for it...thinking outside the box! And here, our happy consultants throw open the doors of our prison and out pops our creative jack-in-the-box.

Peter: So, is there a 6th model?

Adrian: Yes – The talent and perspiration model – Each of the five creativity-cultivation models assume that somewhere and somehow our natural creativity is suppressed. Quite contrary to all that we know about individual differences and human abilities, the assumption is that creativity is not normally distributed: everybody is (potentially) very creative, but creativity may not be a sufficient condition for innovation.

Creativity tips for leaders

Adrian offered ten simple but important ideas:

1. Sleep on it: Come back to problems and issues. Let them fall fallow for a bit; stew; incubate. Revisit them when it suits.
2. Read widely: Talk to all sorts of experts. Get outside your box. Talk to people who think about things differently from you.
3. Don't give up: Persistence is the key. Most attempts fail. Breakthroughs are rare.
4. Take a Risk: Fear of failure, humiliation, teasing and abuse are natural enemies of creativity. Go on – play

with hunches and tentative ideas. Break the rules. Take courage.

5. Piggy-back: Take others' work and take it further. Put things together which do not fit.

6. Identify peak times and conditions: Work out when and where you are at your best for idea generation and refinement. Set aside these times for those activities.

7. Record your flashes: Have a place and method to record all ideas - some worth revisiting and incubation

8. Build your particular expertise/skill/knowledge: creativity is always skill based. Get to the cutting edge of your chosen area... there is no substitute for this.

9. Question and Probe the obvious: Take little for granted; turn things upside down; celebrate similarities and differences.

10. Lighten up: Be playful; use humour; have a sense of the absurd and the ridiculous.

Editor's note: Check also the work of Jane Henry and Professor Charles Handy in the article on The Beatles.

Adrian Furnham may be contacted via his website www.adrianfurnham.com

"Two different things:

    A crowd is a tribe without a
    leader

    A crowd is a tribe without
    communication

Most organisations spend their
time marketing to the crowd.
Smart organisations assemble
the tribe"

Seth Godin

The 3 Rs of Leadership: Rachmaninov, Reinhardt and the Rolling Stones

In an attempt to rethink business after the worst recession for many decades, it is vital to rethink leadership and the sorts of strategies that will help companies thrive and survive. Here we explore three musical genres and their connections and contrasts with leadership. It offers a review of leadership postures, as seen through three diverse forms of music: orchestras; jazz bands and; rock music, typified by 3 stereotypes or the 3Rs: Rachmaninov; Reinhardt and; The Rolling Stones.

In the beginning there were orchestras ...

Through the industrial age many people have led companies as though they were orchestras. Obsessed by the need for order and control in the way work should be organised, they created structures into which people were fitted. "Paint it Black" as Henry Ford would have said (but not "Mellow Yellow" or "A Whiter Shade of Pale"...:-). This meant that one person (the conductor/leader) held the composer's operating instructions (the score).

The performer's/employee's main role was to follow the score accurately and without deviation (improvisation). This analogy has been attractive through the industrial age for the following reasons:

• It gave leaders a feeling of absolute control and certainty about the future. This enabled them to make plans about the future based on the past.

- It gave followers certainty about their role and required performance levels. Fixed job descriptions and performance management methods provide a rhythm and routine to daily life. Over time, such systems become 'unconscious structures' or 'scores' that create conformity and level performance to acceptable rather than extraordinary levels.
- It gave shareholders a sense of direction and trust in the business strategy. Relatively few people want to buy shares in a company where the CEO stands up at the AGM and quotes the lines of "Blockbuster" by glam pop band The Sweet: "Does anyone know the way?" Shareholder expectation contributes to the idea that leaders need to know their own mind and be in control in an age of uncertainty, when, often, nothing could be further from the truth.

The orchestra analogy is essentially about conformity in terms of 'getting it right' and collaboration around a set of instructions, in other words 'doing what you are told'. Group identity is more important than individual stardom in an orchestra with certain exceptions. The main questions an orchestra must ask itself are: "Did we get it right?" and "Did we give a good rendition of the composer's idea?"

The orchestra analogy is useful at work when: The business environment and product/service mix is simple and stable and; staff expectations of work and its meaning are consistent. But, how many enterprises fit this profile in the 21st Century? It also assumes that the conductor (the CEO) has the right sheet music, is supremely good at conducting and that the orchestra members are very good at following a pre-planned score. The orchestra analogy is increasingly out of step with the way that innovative businesses get things done, because the CEO usually does not and cannot know everything required for establishing a top down strategy. In the information age Dr Daniel Levitin estimates that we take in five times as much data in 2011 than we did in 1986 and we process 34 GB of data daily. Against such a background, at best leaders only have some of the sheet music, or, even worse, might be using an outdated score. They may also be better at playing than conducting.

... and then there was jazz

John Kao noted the connections between jazz and leadership in his book "Jamming: The Art and Discipline of Business Creativity". He points out that creativity is fuelled by contradictions: between discipline and freedom; convention and experiment; old and new; familiar and strange; expert and naïve; power and desire. Kao points out that leaders should not try to resolve contradictions but work with them. This is very valuable advice indeed.

However, Kao's vision is mostly about genius level creativity. He uses Charlie Parker amongst his examples of successful freeform jazz musicians who operates at the 'edge of chaos'. You must be a brilliant player to be able to do this and this points to one difficulty with the jazz analogy at work; that much business creativity is quite ordinary and does not always require or value genius level contributions. Have you ever tried to get experts to work together in a University? It's analogous to a supergroup, where the collective brainpower and egos of the various players make the mixture so volatile that the group frequently implodes. So, what is the middle ground?

Peter Cook   www.academy-of-rock.co.uk

Let there be rock

Both the orchestra and the jazz analogies offer us complementary insights into leadership. The rock music analogy is essentially about breaking away from the score and doing your own thing but within the context of the overall structure, as endless improvisation and creativity are wasteful in terms of successful innovation. Unlike an orchestra, the individual is as important as the team in a rock band, although there are some star soloists. The main questions a successful rock band must ask itself are: "Did we stand out from the crowd?" and "How was the performance?"

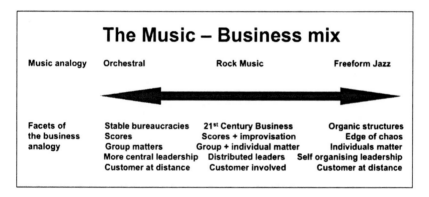

The Music – Business mix

Music analogy	Orchestral	Rock Music	Freeform Jazz
Facets of the business analogy	Stable bureaucracies Scores Group matters More central leadership Customer at distance	21st Century Business Scores + improvisation Group + individual matter Distributed leaders Customer involved	Organic structures Edge of chaos Individuals matter Self organising leadership Customer at distance

These are rather similar to the questions that 21st century companies must ask: "What difference does it make?" and "What do our customers think of us?" Here is a comparison of the three models with parallels for companies and organisations seeking to balance their approach to leadership:

The rock music analogy is looser than the orchestra analogy, but not so chaotic as to need the genius level approach required in the jazz analogy. It occupies the middle ground, which is where most 21st Century Businesses are, both tight and loose, both the team and the individuals matter, leaders at all levels, the customer is involved and engaged...

As a new generation of leaders emerge from the tipping point of the financial meltdown and recession, they will need to have new ideas about leading and managing people. This requires:

- Both structure and improvisation.
- Both control and creativity.
- Both team and individual excellence.
- Both individual and group recognition and reward.

The leader's role will be to design best-fit strategies that help leaders to achieve exceptional performances under conditions of inherent uncertainty and rapid change.

"The Boss showed up – and I, one of Earth's newest Bruce groupies by midnight, was mesmerised by the most amazing piece of performance art of any sort I've ever seen (65.8 years) or ever expect to see"

Tom Peters on Bruce Springsteen

Leaders need followers not fans

I'd like you to think that I spent years researching the above quote on leadership and followership. I'd like you to think that, but it would be a dirty lie ...

In fact, I thought the quote up in the shower one morning. I often use the shower as a means of coming up with ideas for my writing, alongside re-pointing walls, swimming and other "low mental energy tasks". The Vice President of Research & Development at Pfizer thought my "leadership shower quote" was so profound that he bought a copy of one of my books on the strength of it and attempted to hire me to come to New York. Because he felt so strongly about the quote, I did not have the heart to tell him that I thought of it in the smallest room of our house and not the biggest library in a noted University. But time changes everything, so I now feel able to reveal my "dirty secret". See the picture for the quote.

The thought came to me because casual observers of what I do think that I'm saying that business leaders need to be like rock stars. Nothing could be further from the truth, but it's a well-trodden path. The BBC tried to place me in the "Rock Star as Leader" corner when they interviewed me for Radio 4. Several University Professors have devised "Leadership and Rock Star" seminars to try to make their lectures more interesting, even though they should know that leadership is a team game. Even respected journalists have penned articles alluding to the idea that leaders should be more about style than substance.

Peter Cook   www.academy-of-rock.co.uk

Hooked?

Creative leaders encourage followers, not 'fans'.
Fans will follow you over a cliff. Followers will tell you
before it's too late!

Peter Cook

The notion that leaders should be like the popular idea of a rock star does not work for several reasons:

1. Nobody wants to work for an emotionally bankrupt, narcissistic boss in the business world. The popular models put up like "The Apprentice" bear little relation for the host of great people I've worked for in my career. Never forget that The Apprentice is just entertainment!

2. Leaders get nothing from behaving like rock stars either in the long run. By having fans, they run the risk of never receiving any helpful feedback if they are about to go over a cliff! A good follower is not so frightened of the leader that they feel unable to tell them something difficult, dangerous or downright diabolical. I have been very fortunate to have had many great leaders and mentors in my time, although I accept that this is not everybody's experience, through the plethora of posts about "bad bosses" on social media.

3. In the music business, some of the greatest rock stars I've met are fully in touch with their feelings, their audiences and lack any sense of hubris or narcissism. Time after time, when meeting music giants like Roberta Flack, George Clinton, John Mayall, Bill Nelson, Bernie Tormé, Nigel Kennedy, Patti Russo et al, I find that truly great people in the music business are not like the "rock star" myth that prevails in the media. Of course there are exceptions to every rule and I won't name names here!

What great thoughts have you had in the shower?

Peter Cook   www.academy-of-rock.co.uk

"Leaders need followers not fans. Fans will follow you over a cliff. Followers will tell you before it's too late"

Peter Cook

Classical Gas: Leadership lessons from Nigel Kennedy

I went to see Nigel Kennedy at a concert celebrating the work of composers that filled his early years, from Bach to Fats Domino. Featuring a simple four piece of virtuoso musicians from Poland I had the great pleasure of meeting Nigel after the show. He was astonished that I'd noticed a cheeky and subtle reference to the blues harmonica embedded in one of his classical jazz pieces within the 90-minute performance (probably just a couple of seconds of playing) and invited me for drinks as a result. But the real question for me and you is, what can leaders learn from Nigel Kennedy?

Personal Leadership

Nigel is a thoroughly warm and authentic individual who refuses to be classified by others and who is equally comfortable mixing with royalty and those in the gutter staring at the stars. At the age of 16, he faced threats from his classical tutors, when he was offered the chance to play with Stéphane Grappelli at New York's Carnegie Hall, saying that it would be the end of his classical career. He refused to heed the threats and crossed the invisible line between the classics and jazz. He has subsequently played material by Jimi Hendrix and The Doors, giving the establishment a run for their money. These qualities are what business academic Rosabeth Moss-Kanter called a 'boundary crosser' and what Gareth Jones termed an 'authentic chameleon'. Kennedy shares this unwillingness to be classified with the Prince, who has also systematically crossed musical genres, testing his audience's patience to destruction at times.

Peter Cook   www.academy-of-rock.co.uk

Team Leadership

Kennedy works with a trio of musicians who he met in jazz jam sessions in his new home town of Krakow. Just watching the band work through his set was an exemplar of what I call 'planned spontaneity', which is itself a core competence for leaders who often face extremes of uncertainty in their businesses. Too much planning stiffens the performance. Too much spontaneity makes the performance sloppy. Like most things in life, it's a clever balance. What other transferable lessons from Kennedy's musical performance can we learn?

Simplicity – The drummer used one snare drum for much of the performance, using every part of the instrument and his hands to gain an enormous range of sounds from one drum. This is the work of a true master. The same principle applies in the world of innovation. A major factor that prevents new ideas from reaching the market is complexity. In a busy world if your new product or service cannot be explained imply and succinctly, you are much less likely to be able to diffuse the product into popular usage. In the words of Einstein "Things should be made as simple as possible, but no simpler."

Interplay – Although it was obvious to me that the show had been extensively rehearsed, the true joy of the performance was when Nigel signalled the guitar player to extend his solos, during 'interruptions' of the performance by Nigel who was cajoling the drummer and bass player mid stream. This is incredibly difficult to describe in print so you must catch him and the band on tour. The point of the matter is that great team leaders inspire the team to greater levels of performance by a combination of pre-planned and some spontaneous challenges

www.academy-of-rock.co.uk   Peter Cook

to keep performances fresh. It's a trait I've also observed at close range, when performing Bernie Tormé and with 'two hit wonder and punk idol' John Otway who we looked at earlier in this book. All masters of their art and live examplars of what I call 'prepared spontaneity'.

Timing – Nigel's band has exquisite timing, and this allows them to perform various musical acrobatics. This is as the result of a combination of individual genius and what Tom Peters and others have dubbed the 10000 hours effect. Timing is an entirely transferable and largely overlooked part of a leader's repertoire. Smart leaders choose their moment to intervene on complex or difficult issues in the same way that an improvising musician makes choices over when to play and when to

Not exactly Two Pints of Lager and a Packet of Crisps...

remain silent. When do you leave a space in the conversation at a meeting for other soloists to contribute?

Teamwork – Given the size of the egos and capabilities in Nigel's ensemble, the miracle of teamwork is that all manage to leave their egos in the dressing room, playing off one another in a true example of what can happen of how healthy competition leads to peak performance. It is rare to get teams of experts to collaborate in such a way in a musical setting and just as rare in business. Just think of all the 'supergroups' that have imploded through the ages. The smart leader is responsible for ensuring that diversity is truly valued and that all pay attention to all, all the time, so that they may take the performance higher.

Brand Leadership

Nigel Kennedy has extended his influence across many fields and the testimony to this could be seen by a casual look around the audience, who comprised well-heeled theatre-goers through to rock fans, perhaps of lesser means. Very few artists could command such a demographic.

Whilst Nigel Kennedy has a clearly identifiable brand, he has refused to be sub-categorised by marketers who like to 'thin-slice' a brand in an ambition to provide seemingly greater 'coherence'. Kennedy is living proof that marketing plans are not the only way to have a great brand.

Five Lessons for Leaders

1. Be yourself completely, regardless of who you are with.

2.   Dare to be different. Ensure that your 'difference' brings exceptional value if dealing with established viewpoints.

3.   Keep things simple when taking something new to the market.

4.   Ensure the team is both challenged and understands the value of play. Leave egos at the door when collaborating.

5.   Avoid the trap of thin slicing your brand so that it loses broader appeal.

Must the show go on?

I've just come back from a weekend with the Godfather of Neuro-Linguistic Programming (NLP), Dr Richard Bandler and stage hypnotist Paul McKenna. At one point during the weekend, the song "The Show Must Go On" popped up in the back of my mind. Undoubtedly this maxim pervades most entertainment circles. Does it transfer to business I thought? I felt a certain unease ...

I'd argue vigorously that the maxim is at least unhelpful and possibly dangerous in some circumstances. One of my great business heroes Tom Peters, points out that one of the hardest things to do in business is press the STOP button. In rock circles, my friend Bill Nelson has a maxim for reinvention that says "Do not be afraid of the off switch". Had Michael Jackson written the song "Wanna Be Stoppin' Somethin'" rather than "Wanna Be Startin' Somethin'", it would have probably not been a hit however, ha ha!

Peter Cook

But the STOP button is vital in some circumstances. Kodak would have probably avoided Chapter 11 bankruptcy if they had made the switch from analogue to digital film sooner. Especially so, since Kodak pioneered digital camera technology. We explore this a little further in the article on Bill Nelson later on in this book. This is proof positive of the old adage, "The last thing a fish notices is the water that surrounds it".

Even great companies like Sony might have avoided a steady decline in their innovation fortunes if they had recognised the advent of downloading and done something different with their record company rather than pretending the problem would go away. Sony was thought to be one of the most innovative companies 20 years ago, with a continuous stream of innovations, then somehow they lost the muse and it took many years to recover.

In our personal lives, great leaders ask themselves dangerous questions, such as:

- What things are we doing that we really should not, just out of habit?
- What things are we accidentally, deliberately or perversely avoiding?

I can think of quite a few things that need to go in my 'life laundry'. I have reviewed my business on a yearly basis for over 20 years and commit certain strategies and ambitions to the waste bin to make space for new things. Of course, it's much harder to stop the momentum in larger businesses and therefore much more necessary to work hard at it. How do you do it?

Peter Cook   www.academy-of-rock.co.uk

A periodic pause for reflection before moving on is a healthy part of any smart person's business and personal life. Contact me for a free consultation if you need to do your personal or business life laundry. "STOP In The Name Of Life" may not have been a hit for Diana Ross but it may improve your bank balance!

Questions to ponder

1. What activities and habits are you pursuing that are past their sell-by date?
2. What 'dark alleyways' do others lead you down that do not contribute to your overall life purpose?
3. What relationships or tasks are you pursuing that are not based on a sense of equity/reciprocity? How can you change them so that they produce better results for all?
4. What strategies or tactics are you pursuing that would benefit from better timing? Can you put them into the recycler for a time when they are more likely to succeed?
5. What business activities are in need of some 'fermentation' before you launch them on an unsuspecting world?
6. How might you go faster by slowing down?

"Music is the language of the emotions"

Leo Tolstoy

I Get Knocked Down,
But I Get Up Again ...

Leaders and some entrepreneurs share what I call the 'Chumbawamba effect' in common. Check out the song "Tubthumping" on YouTube by punk folk group Chumbawamba to hear what I mean.

The lyric "I get knocked down but I get up again" summarises the quality of 'emotional resilience' or 'mental toughness'. Emotional resilience is defined as an individual's ability to cope with stress and adversity. Accepted wisdom says that the ability to recover from life's difficulties and move on is a good thing. Certainly it's a very important concept for creative people and innovators as life throws its fair degree of obstacles in the way of a new idea. In my time working on life-saving pharmaceuticals, I've seen brilliant scientists destroyed by changes of plans for drug research and development, which mean that they are asked to stop working on their pet project or passion. There is a marked difference between those individuals that see such changes pragmatically for what they are, i.e. a change in priorities and those who see these changes as a personal attack on their soul and identity. Bouncing back may take years in such extreme cases. This is clearly not productive for the person or the enterprise.

At the other extreme we have those who keep bouncing back but who never learn from their mistakes. Typified by people who start an enterprise, fail, make themselves bankrupt, start up again the following day and keep doing this, leaving chaos and disorder in their wake. These people are popularised by some media people as entrepreneurs, yet in my humble opinion they are just charlatans and cheats. The stereotype is characterised by the deeply ironic comic failure Alan Partridge, who continuously covers up successive repetitive failures and a gradual decline into oblivion in an hilarious way. Check Alan Partridge out on DVD if you are not familiar with this comic genius. Like most great comedy, the scripts are appallingly funny since they are based on creative exaggerations of real life.

Make sure your hard hat does not stop you from listening and learning

The point of Chumbawamba's title, reset in the context of big psychological ideas, is that, if you hit an obstacle, setback or failure in your work or life, the most important thing is to learn from that experience. Paradoxically, a high level of skill in the area of self-awareness can be just as dangerous as having none of this quality.

• Those with high self-awareness may drown in regret/reflection/rumination when they hit a setback.

Peter Cook   www.academy-of-rock.co.uk

- Those without high self-awareness may continue crashing through life regardless of their own and other's expense. As David Bowie put it "Always Crashing In The Same Car".

Failure is part of the entrepreneur's toolkit, but it should not be repetitive. One definition of insanity is doing the same thing and expecting a different result.

The differentiator is the ability to learn from setbacks and move on, carrying the lessons with you. That's a smart way to deal with failure. Once you have learned, shut up and move on.

Sir Richard Branson is an excellent example of someone with huge amounts of experience, but who also knows the value of remaining fresh and open, listening to ideas and accepting that failure is a natural part of progress. Branson is a hard-headed decision maker but someone who has not let experience harden his ability to listen and learn. It's worth a read of his book "The Virgin Way" for an insight into emotional intelligence at a practical level.

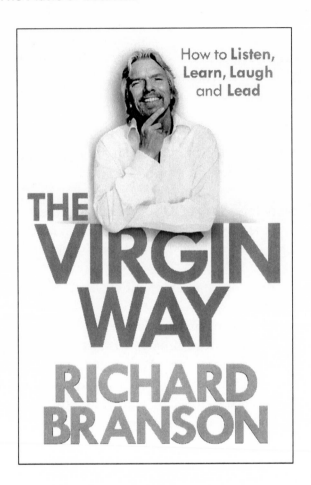

"I've been knocked down a
number of times"

James Brown

Like a Virgin: Madonna on reinvention

Madonna rocketed to stardom so quickly in 1984 that it obscured most of her musical virtues. Appreciating her music became even more difficult later on, as her lifestyle became more of a talking point than her music. However, Madonna manipulated the media and the public with her music, her videos, her publicity, and her sexuality. Arguably, Madonna was the first female pop star to have complete control of her music and image. Whether we approve of her means, we can't deny that she has made a huge impact on the world. Britney Spears, Katy Perry, Beyoncé, Lady Gaga and a host of others have learned much from Madonna.

But what about her reinvention and leadership qualities? To find out the roots of what makes someone the person they are, it's often a good idea to look back to someone's early life and their personality. In Madonna's case, a number of critical moments in her life are probably instrumental in shaping her character. Her mother died of cancer when Madonna was five years old, leaving behind unresolved feelings of anger, guilt etc. This seems to have produced a great deal of determination later on. Madonna studied hard at school to ensure she would get on. At the same time, there was unresolved conflict with her father, who married the housekeeper. These formative experiences would set a context for the person Madonna became as she acquired stardom.

In psychological terms, Madonna is an ESTP in terms of her Myers Briggs personality type. That's E for Extrovert, S for

Sensing, T for Thinker and P for Perceiver. Broadly speaking this makes her a gregarious networker, someone who enjoys logic, putting objectivity above personal feelings and someone who likes to keep their options open. ESTPs are also good with details and often unprepared to compromise.

I suspect this is part of what has made Madonna such a good business woman, as she does not let personal feelings get in the way of tough decisions. This contrasts well with many artists and musicians who are weighed down by their feelings about their work and let these cloud any business decisions they might wish to take. In extremis, this explains why many artists don't always make a commercial success of their art. I constantly meet musicians who find it impossible to separate their feelings from hard decisions that will affect their future. This does seem to be both the charm and curse of being a musician. In my view, Bill Nelson is a classic 'NF' in Myers Briggs terms, i.e. an intuitive feeler. This makes him more vulnerable to manipulation by music business executives and he has indeed suffered at the hands of the vampiric music industry. We learn more about Mr Nelson in the next chapter.

Madonna has reinvented herself several times, kept her existing audiences and acquired new ones. This is the trick that all businesses need to pull off rather than becoming 'one hit wonders'.

In the music business, it is more usual to reinvent yourself and lose your audience or be a 'one hit wonder'. Starting out as a disco diva with songs like "Holiday" and "Physical Attraction", Madonna established herself as an international star via her 1984 album "Like a Virgin". She quickly consolidated her position through her music, fashion and publicity, which even caused the Pope to tell his followers not to go to Madonna's concerts. This was a major coup d'etat to gain this much disapproval from the establishment and one wonders just whether this was a calculated move or simply a stroke of luck. It's one thing to have a large record company on your side for marketing, quite another to have the head of the Catholic Church in charge of your PR!

"Losing my virginity was a career move" Madonna

Madonna has reinvented herself a number of times in her career, taking her audience with her in every case:

- Sex goddess – Madonna published the controversial 'Sex' book. In doing so, she defied the wishes of her record company, demonstrating that it was her and not her record company in charge of her direction.
- Serious actress – Madonna was acclaimed for her roles in Evita, which was nominated for five academy awards.
- Champion for Africa – In the last few years Madonna has championed a number of causes for Africa, making an impact that politicians only dream of.
- Classy ballad singer – Madonna was often ignored as a serious singer due to her other high profile activity. She shows herself to be a classy ballad singer. Many of her best songs in this style were brought together in her album "Something To Remember".
- R&B/urban pop star – Madonna has partnered with much younger R&B/urban pop stars, such as Justin Timberlake and Timbaland, pulling off the trick that eludes many people of her generation.

The norm in music is to reinvent yourself at the expense of your audience. Madonna, Bowie and a few others are the exception that proves this rule. In business the story is similar. Stora Enso issued their first share in 1288. Japan has a small number of companies that are more than 1,000 years old. Most of these companies share a core value that success is not solely tied to profit making.

However these examples are very much the exception with the average lifetime of a business being of the order of 25 years and falling in an age of turbulent markets and unfaithful customers.

"I have the same goal I've had ever since I was a girl: I want to rule the world"

Madonna Ciccone

Bat Out Of Hell: Career coaching for Rock Stars

I've been doing some Coaching with Patti Russo to assist her with career reinvention and renewal, now that she is pursing a solo portfolio career. Patti was Meatloaf's long term singing partner for 20 years, having worked with Cher, Queen, Bryan Ferry, Betty Harris and the Trans-Siberian Orchestra, to name a few. She is also no stranger to the theatre stage, having appeared as Esmeralda in the London production of Notre-Dame de Paris and as Killer Queen in the Las Vegas production of Queen and Ben Elton's smash hit musical We Will Rock You. How then do you set about coaching someone on a portfolio career when they themselves have made their own way through their life, having dealt with some of the most passionate people with the largest egos on the planet?

Coaching crucially depends on what I call a good "psychological contract":

- There must be excellent rapport and chemistry between the coach and the client.
- There must be an important client goal to pursue for which there is no obvious and easy solution.
- The client must believe that the coach is in a position to help.
- The coach must have a wide repertoire of skills and experience to draw upon to fit the client's preferred style.

I'm pleased to say that Patti was pure joy to work with in this respect. This was particularly pleasing as she takes no prisoners

Peter Cook   www.academy-of-rock.co.uk

and we did not have a great deal of time!! Here's the process we used:

1. We started out by mapping out Patti's life. This revealed a number of patterns and more importantly potential connections to assist in the next phase.

2. From this, a series of goals emerged. Our psychological contract was for me to actively provoke as well as just support her. In short we used the full range of coaching styles available. It would have been a mistake to go for the goals first without the background and career and life mapping approach. I hold John Heron's model in my head as a kind of useful "compass" to help me determine

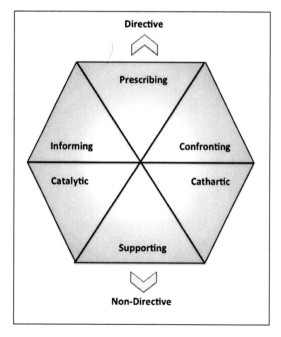

A helpful model

what the client needs most and used most of the styles available in an intuitive way on reflection.

3. Through a series of follow up sessions, we then "joined up the dots", actually making connections as we went. It's the old adage "The longest journey starts with the smallest step". This included some cathartic purging of stuff in the longest coaching car journey ever undertaken as I drove Patti back from Henley to London late one evening after a performance at the Business School. Clearance is necessary if you are to make space for new things.

4. Like all good coaching, it rests with the person themselves to do the hard work and I'm delighted to report that Patti has set herself on a course towards realising her

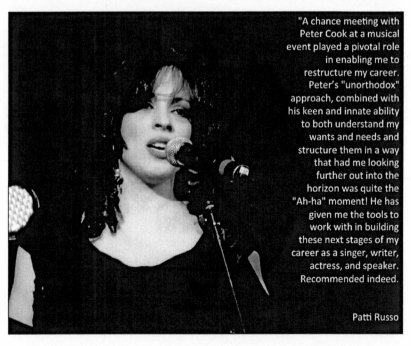

"A chance meeting with Peter Cook at a musical event played a pivotal role in enabling me to restructure my career. Peter's "unorthodox" approach, combined with his keen and innate ability to both understand my wants and needs and structure them in a way that had me looking further out into the horizon was quite the "Ah-ha" moment! He has given me the tools to work with in building these next stages of my career as a singer, writer, actress, and speaker. Recommended indeed.

Patti Russo

Peter Cook   www.academy-of-rock.co.uk

aspirations. Whilst Patti is best known for her singing and acting, as a result of this she has decided to develop a wider but linked portfolio for the next stage of her career.

Alongside her role as a singer-songwriter and actress, Patti's career portfolio now also includes some new options:

Inspirational speaking – Patti is a credible and passionate speaker. Henley had this to say about our first joint event:

> *Q: What do you get when you cross leadership development with rock music? A: Peter Cook and his Academy of Rock! Peter and his team provided an excellent finale to the Henley Business School Open Leadership Programme (where I was one of the tutor team). He provided an engaging, fun and memorable evening session drawing the parallels between the challenges and skills of a first class leader and a rock musician. The session tapped into the emotions and liberated even the more introverted to let their hair down. A real example of how to engage your team and showcase their talents!*

TV and Media appearances – We are currently pursuing a number of avenues to develop Patti's career in these areas.

Writing – Patti's story is a true tale of "gypsies, tramps and thieves", to quote Cher, starting out with nothing and climbing to the top. She got her job with Meatloaf by answering an anonymous ad in the Village Voice in NYC and had experienced several knock backs before that. There's a book somewhere in this …

If you ever have to coach someone, make sure that you set the conditions for success at the outset. Preparation is all.

Bill Nelson, personal mastery and reinvention

In this article we examine the question of personal reinvention. Not through the usual business suspects, but through the example of the music legend Bill Nelson. You might be wondering, just who is Bill Nelson? And what can a rock star teach us about personal reinvention? How is that relevant for us in our lives and work? We will start with some background.

Bill Nelson with "Orchestra Futura" – Dave Sturt and Theo Travis
Photo © Martin Bostock

Bill Nelson led 70s Art School band Be-Bop Deluxe and Red Noise. In spite of his huge success, Nelson left considerable wealth and fame to pursue his own artistic and musical direction. However, like so many great influencers, his footprint on modern music is immense and pervasive. Nelson is admired

www.academy-of-rock.co.uk   Peter Cook

by a catalogue of rock's monarchy, including McCartney, Brian May, Kate Bush, Brian Eno, David Sylvian, Prince, The Foo Fighters, The Darkness and so on.

I was astonished and amazed to discover that Lady Starlight loves Bill's work and has been using one of his songs "Darkness L'immoraliste" in her performance art act on Lady Gaga's world tour. Perhaps it's time to update Gaga with Bill's extensive catalogue for her next jazz album after the Tony Bennett era?

Bill Nelson articulated his principles for personal creativity and reinvention his book "Diary of a Hyperdreamer". Although they are artistically expressed and therefore not written in the kind of business jargon most of us are familiar with, they are directly transferable to the world of business. Bill kindly allowed me to do some 'translation and here's the full list with one or two of them expanded upon:

Bill Nelson's reinvention principles

1. Be afraid of neither the future nor the past but make a mark on the moment.
2. Do not give in to the temptation to elicit favour.
3. Resist the obvious but embrace it when it becomes perverse to do so.
4. When gazing in the mirror, look for the artist rather than the guitarist.
5. Build a bridge between melody and dissonance.
6. Do not be afraid of the 'off' switch.
7. Hang no hopes or importance on your actions.
8. Act only when there are no alternatives to stasis.
9. When no words appear, refuse to sing.
10. Ignore all extraneous noise.
11. Cease to seduce.
12. Trust the muse, she always knows best.

Here's some of Bill's principles translated:

Principle 4. Look for the artist rather than the guitarist

'When gazing in the mirror, look for the artist rather than the guitarist' relates to the business of making good choices. What implicit or explicit criteria do you or your business use to assess temptations? Do you have a clear idea of the difference between the 'artist', i.e. who you are and why you are on planet

Earth and the 'guitarist' – what you do for a living, to keep yourself occupied and so on? Is there a link between 'who' and 'what'?

Leaders need to constantly refer themselves back to the vital questions: 'What business am I really in? And what is this business here for?' They then devise a strategy that connects what is done to the higher purpose, rather than a series of disconnected expedient moves. Art and Business are really not so far apart in this regard.

Principle 6. Don't fear the 'off' switch

Nelson's 'off' switch is curious. What could this mean in business terms? Is this the ultimate distinction between art and

business? Many businesses would be better off if they were to adopt this principle, i.e. stopping things that are no longer wanted or needed rather than just carrying on regardless. There is often an irresistible temptation to continue in the face of compelling evidence that there is a need to do something different.

Kodak experienced this with the death of conventional film processing. Had they chosen to respond to the trend some years back, they might have been in a better position to respond to market change. Having now filed for Chapter 11 bankruptcy, Kodak does not even have Sony's excuse that they were committed to analogue rather than digital technology. After all, Kodak pioneered digital photography. They badly misjudged the rate at which the world would respond, thinking that they controlled the market.

Principle 8. Act only when there are no alternatives to stasis

'Acting only when there are no alternatives to stasis' reminds us to examine all alternatives before making a decision on critical issues. This is not a recipe for not making decisions! Examining alternatives requires us to synthesise options, to bring alternatives together that will produce better options rather than compromises. It requires the use of analogue (and/also) thinking rather than digital (on/off) thinking. The pressure of business life often forces us into action rather than reflection/synthesis, with the result that we get sub-optimal decisions and/or performance.

Principle 12. Trust the muse – she knows best

In the context of business reinvention, 'trusting the muse' means that we should trust intuition rather than relying on research as a means of doing new things. We live in a world that is drowning in data. As a result we downplay intuition. Bill Nelson's approach to reinvention values hunch and lunch more than a spreadsheet and Wall Street to predict the future. New stuff does not always come out of a detailed analysis of old stuff! In Bill's case, I think the muse also comes to mean Emiko, his wife – always a wise move to listen to your wife!

These inner recipes for creativity and transformation are rather rare. I'd strongly recommend you check out books such as "The Act of Creation" by Arthur Koestler, "The Creative Process" by Brewster Ghiselin, "Insights of Genius" by Arthur Miller and "The Empty Raincoat" by Professor Charles Handy to learn

Some of Bill Nelson's continuously creative output

Peter Cook   www.academy-of-rock.co.uk

more about the inner creativity process and the process of re-invention.

I am proud to know Bill Nelson, who has integrity and creativity written into his DNA, even at the expense of fame and fortune. Integrity is easy when it does not mean you have to make difficult financial choices, but most people fall by the wayside when the going gets tough.

Check out Bill Nelson's extensive catalogue of music via www.billnelson.com

"Without music, life would be a mistake"

Friedrich Nietzsche

Changes: Reinvention lessons from David Bowie

Compared with all the 'one hit wonders' in music, David Bowie has reinvented himself several times AND taken his audience with him. The parallel lesson in business is that of changing what you do, keeping your customers AND gaining new ones. What can we learn about reinvention from David Bowie?

Lesson # 1. Find a focus

David Bowie began performing music when he was 13 years old, learning the saxophone while he was at High School and began playing in a number of mod bands. All these bands released singles, which were generally ignored, yet he continued performing. The following year, he released the Anthony Newley inspired music hall styled "Laughing Gnome". Upon completing the record, he spent several weeks in a Buddhist monastery. Damn good idea in my opinion, although I should be so lucky to have written this song in spite of its cheesiness!! Once he left the monastery, he formed a mime company – a non-obvious career move. This was short-lived, and he formed an experimental art group in 1969. For me this aligns well with Wallas' 1926 notion of incubation to find your source of creativity.

Lesson # 2. Get good people

Necessity is the mother of invention and Bowie needed to finance the art group, so he signed a record deal. His first album featured "Space Oddity", which became a major hit single in

Britain. He began miming at T. Rex concerts, eventually touring with Marc Bolan's bassist/producer Tony Visconti and guitarist Mick Ronson. The band quickly fell apart, yet Bowie and
Ronson continued to work together. The next album, "The Man
who Sold the World" did not gain much attention. Following
the release of "Hunky Dory", featuring Ronson and keyboardist
Rick Wakeman, Bowie developed his most famous incarnation,
"Ziggy Stardust". Bowie quickly followed Ziggy with "Aladdin
Sane". Not only did he record a new album that year, but he also
produced albums for Lou Reed, Iggy and Mott the Hoople's "All
the Young Dudes", for which he also wrote the title track. It
would perhaps be a stretch of the imagination to suggest that
Bowie would make a great HR manager, but perhaps that is the
essential lesson here: Surround yourself with great people. Do
not be frightened of people who are better than yourself – it
simply helps you get better quicker.

Lesson # 3. Re-engineer

Bowie unexpectedly announced his retirement from live performances during his final show in 1973. He retreated from the
spotlight to work on a musical adaptation of George Orwell's
1984, transforming the work into "Diamond Dogs" and the
hit single "Rebel Rebel". Bowie supported the album with an
American tour. As the tour progressed, Bowie became fascinated with soul music. He subsequently refashioned his group
into a soul band and revamped his image. The change took fans
by surprise. "Young Americans", released in 1975, was the cul-
mination of Bowie's soul obsession. It became his first major
crossover hit, peaking in the American Top Ten and generating

his first U.S. number one hit in "Fame", a song he co-wrote with John Lennon and guitarist Carlos Alomar. Bowie effectively jumped 20 years ahead of Michael Hammer and James Champey and the Business Process Re-engineering (BPR) movement in about 3 months. Being comfortable is never a recipe for success in business. Comfort breeds complacency. Make yourself uncomfortable to keep developing.

Lesson # 4. Challenge sacred cows

Once in Berlin, Bowie began painting, as well as studying art. He also developed a fascination with German electronic music, which Brian Eno helped him fulfill on their first album together, "Low". Released early in 1977, Low was a startling mixture of electronics, pop and avant-garde. It was one of the most influential albums of the late '70s, as was its follow-up, "Heroes". There is a direct link with Peter Senge's seminal work on single and double loop learning here in terms of becoming a Learning Organisation:

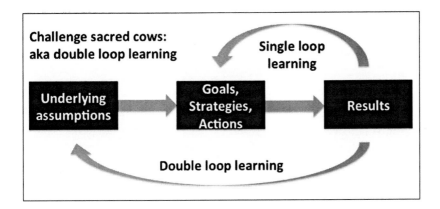

Lesson # 5. Perpetual change

In 1983, he released "Let's Dance". Bowie recruited Chic guitarist Nile Rodgers to produce the album, giving the record a sleek, funky foundation, and hired the unknown Stevie Ray Vaughan as lead guitarist. Let's Dance became his most successful record. HR people talk about change management at length. Bowie just gets on with it. I had the great privilege of meeting Nile Rodgers and explored his part in helping Bowie find the funk with him.

Lesson # 6. Learn from Failure

Bowie's next project was less successful. He formed a guitar rock band called Tin Machine. They released an album to poor reviews and supported it with a small tour, which was only moderately successful. Tin Machine released a second album, "Tin Machine II", which was largely ignored. Tin Machine contained the innovative work of Reeves Gabrels on guitar but was perhaps too far ahead for some people to latch on to. When change does not work it is time to change again ...

Lesson # 7. Partner

Bowie teamed up with Brian Eno to produce "Outside" and went on tour, co-headlining with Nine Inch Nails, to lure a younger audience, but his strategy failed. In 1996, he recorded "Earthling", an album heavily influenced by techno and drum'n'bass. Earthling received positive reviews, yet it did not attract a new audience. Many techno purists criticised Bowie for exploiting their subculture. It seemed that his attempt to cross age and culture divides was not going to work on this occasion. Since then, Bowie has formed partnerships with a number of artists including Placebo and released a major new work in 2013 "The Next Day" to critical acclaim from a new generation as well as the older one.

Summary – Ch Ch Ch Changes

1. Make radical changes even when your current strategy is successful. Bowie's example reminds me of Handy's idea of the double sigmoid curve in 'The Empty Raincoat'.
2. Hire and work with the best people you can find, especially if they are better than you. Put crudely, stand on the shoulders of giants.
3. Become an expert at change and build the ultimate chameleon organisation. It's what the business gurus call the flexible firm.
4. Constantly read the environment and engage with new movements when they are more than fads. Separate fads from long-term future trends.
5. Learn from failure and quickly move on.

"Be the change that you wish
to see in the world"

Mahatma Ghandi

Uptown Funk: the Bruno Mars HR disciplinary

In a slight departure from our overall theme, I just had to include this post from David D'Souza for its creativity and sense of fun and ironic HR wit. It concerns a fictional disciplinary hearing with Bruno Mars, which I love for its sense of fun. There is no point leading an enterprise if it's not fun. You should check the song "Uptown Funk" out on YouTube whilst reading this.

Notes from informal meeting with Bruno Mars

Background: Following recent complaints from colleagues a meeting was arranged with Bruno (BM) to discuss his recent conduct, in particular his language regarding women.

Meeting commenced approx 9.30am

HR: Hi, Bruno, please come in and take a seat. Would you like a glass of water?

BM: What's this about, I'm not really sure why I'm here.

HR: We've had some complaints about your language and your attitude towards women, we wanted to speak to you informally to help understand if there is a problem.

BM: Um...

HR: For instance – and it would be good to get your take on this – apparently you said *"Bitch, say my name you know who*

I am"?

BM: It wasn't in work...

HR: Even so, can you understand how some of your colleagues may have found that offensive? And just to clarify, when you say that 'it wasn't in work' I believe you were getting paid a sizeable commission and under supervision from your producer at the time

BM: Well...

HR: Moving on. Could you explain what you mean by *"Girls hit your hallelujah"*? I was unclear what that meant, but some people have obviously taken some offence to that. Also apparently you continually complain about the air conditioning saying that you are 'so hot that dragons should retire man'? Do you have a thyroid issue?

BM: It doesn't mean anything. It's just, you know, a phrase. It's a song. It's not real.

HR: It seems unlikely that you would continue to repeat it whilst making an 'ooooh' noise if it didn't mean anything? Could you tell us what you were thinking when you were urging girls to *hit their hallelujah*?

BM: Shouldn't I be allowed a representative or something?

HR: We would rather keep this informal currently, but I'd love for you to put my mind at rest regarding the phrase "If you sexy than flaunt it". I realise that it is a conditional statement, but I was wondering if you had reflected on how it would make the people in the organisation who aren't sexy feel? And whether urging people to flaunt it might be encouraging them to break the dress code.

BM: I really hadn't given it much thought. Is this conversation even legal?

HR: It's just an informal chat at this time. On a separate note we would like to raise some concerns that have come to light regarding your conduct over the last 18 months that make us concerned about this being a pattern of behaviour.

BM: Like what?

HR: Well, on a day where we believed you to be working you recorded The Lazy Song including the line *"I'll be lounging on the couch, Just chillin' in my snuggie"* which doesn't incline us to have confidence we can trust you to work remotely. You were also heard to mention the word 'Grenade' in an office environment

BM: In fairness I said that I would take a grenade FOR someone, that can't be seen as a threat.

HR: Do you think it was sensible to mention grenades at all?

Bruno Mars stood up and left the room, slamming the door behind him approx 9.45, meeting closed.

"If you can get humour and seriousness at the same time, you've created a special little thing, and that's what I'm looking for, because if you get pompous, you lose everything"

Paul Simon

Reflections and connections

This book has taken a magical mystery tour around four major business themes: Strategy – both strategic thinking and executing your strategy; Creativity – generating great ideas and developing them; Innovation – new products, services, strategies, branding and internal process improvements; Leadership – personal leadership style, changing minds and behaviour and reinventing yourself and your enterprise.

I've summarised some of the compelling themes under the four headings below. I'll be writing a follow up book and would love to hear your thoughts in due course, with a view to including an article in the next compilation. Contact me with your thoughts at peter@academy-of-rock.co.uk

Strategy is no longer just about rigid plans and Gantt charts to execute your strategies. In a turbulent world, strategy is a continuous process of reconnaissance, involving colleagues, clients, customers and competitors. Execution of strategy is also about responsiveness and the ability to change course in midstream, whilst avoiding being blown off course by the myriad of business fads that bedevil the business landscape these days. Sticking to the knitting may work for AC/DC, Status Quo and The Rolling Stones, but only in cases where a stable and unchanging market exists.

The smart leader knows that they still haven't found what they're looking for and makes continual improvement part of business as usual. Experimentation with new business models is part of the fabric of modern business strategy, as practiced by the Kaiser Chiefs and Radiohead. When changing, it is important to remember that people are creatures of habit and enjoy change when it rests on important cultural signifiers from the past. This is especially important when working across international cultures, where we need to learn and respect cultural signs and signifiers rapidly if we are to succeed in a global marketplace. Finally, learning from failure is always valuable, especially when it's someone else's failure as with our exploration of Spinal Tap and strategic mis-management.

Creativity and structure are bedfellows of successful improvising rock and jazz combos, as per the examples of Deep Purple and Scott McGill. In business, too much creativity does not lead to profitable and sustainable innovation. Some businesses prefer 'safe creativity' in the form of adaptive ideas. The comparison between Hendrix and Clapton offers a stark contrast in terms of radical versus incremental creativity.

Constraints are not a hindrance to creativity. Indeed constraints can be a spur to ingenious thinking. There are many helpful principles and tools that assist creativity such as the ones put forward by Brian Eno in his Oblique Strategies card deck. Often it pays to customise the approaches for creativity the situation and people tat must use them if you want to engage people beyond a superficial brainstorming event.

Personal creativity benefits from getting in the 'flow' a condition often experienced by master craftspeople in their field. On the other hand we learned from punk rock that naivety is also a place where creative ideas flourish via the story of "Two Pints of Lager and a Packet of Crisps". This point is echoed by punk marketer Richard Laermer, who prefers intuitive approaches to market research and marketing over endless focus groups and surveys.

Innovation is complex and rarely the preserve of the lone inventor or creative person these days. Lady Gaga and Prince offered us insights into how to convert your ideas into profitable innovations. In particular these artists have learned from the feet of giants and improved upon their strategies for success. In some cases innovators are ahead of their audiences. The examples of Marc Bolan, The Velvet Underground and Richard Strange, the godfather of punk, are instructive here. Strange watched The Sex Pistols from the wings of a gig after they had asked to support The Doctors of Madness on tour in 1975. At that point he realised that he was two years too early in launching the punk revolution.

Leaders are also responsible for removing barriers to intrapreneurship. Leaders such as Sir Richard Branson are good exemplars of people who encourage innovation inside their companies.

In Steve Jobs' case as an innovator, he had sufficient business clout to carry his audience with him into new territories. Other innovators, such as Vigier guitars have to be content with a smaller market share when competing with dominant players such as Fender, who innovated in both product and design.

Design is not just the preserve of tangible products. It is also part of good organisation design if you want new things to happen. We learned that opulence does not always create a climate of innovation from my hard rock friend Bernie Tormé and the value of the physical and psychological environment in terms of generating a climate where innovation can happen.

Leadership excellence requires a mastery of ones own values, both in terms of maintaining stability and encouraging change. There is no greater change master than Bill Nelson in this respect, who has pursued a career of continuous creativity in music.

On the popular front, Madonna and David Bowie are expert chameleons: changing; taking their existing audiences with them and; gaining new ones. Changing requires single loop and double loop learning. Any type of learning requires a degree of open-ness to feedback. This is commonly called emotional intelligence by psychologists. Professor Adrian Furnham points out that there is a dark side to the emotional intelligence movement, when leaders become so sensitive to the views of others that they become paralysed in terms of making bold decisions. Nonetheless, the 'Chumbawamba' effect of bouncing back is vital for entrepreneurs and change agents who face setbacks.

However, it's sometimes the STOP button is the most valuable asset a leader has in helping an enterprise turn a difficult corner. It's a lesson that Patti Russo has learned well in her reinvention. STOP, learn, regroup and change. In the words of REM:

"It's the end of the world as we know it, and I feel fine"

Peter Cook   www.academy-of-rock.co.uk

"The greatest danger in times of turbulence is not the turbulence; it is to act with yesterday's logic"

Peter Drucker

About the Author

Peter Cook leads Human Dynamics and The Academy of Rock, a creativity and innovation management consultancy. Business and Organisation Development, Training and Coaching plus Keynotes which blend leading ideas on business with the power of music, be it rock, jazz or classical. Peter delivers keynotes and masterclasses to some of the world's top businesses, including Johnson and Johnson, BP, Pfizer, Laing O'Rourke, Roche, The UN and Imperial College London.

Author of 8 books, including *Sex, Leadership and Rock'n'Roll,* acclaimed by Professor Charles Handy, Harvey Goldsmith and Tom Peters. Peter appears on BBC TV/Radio, Bloomberg TV, The FT, Independent et al. He has an award for his work from Sir Richard Branson and writes for Virgin.com

Peter has followed three concurrent passions over 30 years: science; business and music:

Peter Cook   www.academy-of-rock.co.uk

- Leading innovative Pharmaceutical Product Research and Development teams to bring multi-million dollar life-saving drugs safely to the market including the first treatment for AIDS
- Trouble-shooting businesses and starting up factories around the world
- Internal business, organisation development and change consultancy
- Writing and tutoring for Business Schools at MBA level for blue chips
- Writing and performing music

Peter is an MBA, Chartered Chemist, Chartered Marketer, FCIPD and an NLP Old Master. He works with Duke Corporate Education to offer world class Corporate Development Programmes, ranked No. 1 in the world for 12 years by The FT.

He is also an accomplished rock, pop and jazz musician, having performed alongside Bernie Tormé, John Otway, Wilko Johnson, The Fall and Patti Russo, Meatloaf's long-term singing partner and performer with Queen and Cher. He sponsored 'The Real Spinal Tap Tour' - an entrepreneurial adventure to go on a record breaking rock'n'roll world tour with 'punk idol and two hit wonder' John Otway – The tour was an unmitigated disaster, but the story of this comedy of errors has powerful transferable lessons for entrepreneurs and leaders.

Peter's talks can be accompanied by a roster of class A rock stars and session musicians, with pedigrees performing with

Roger Waters, Mike Oldfield, Ozzy Osbourne, Ian Gillan, The
The Damned, Queen, Meatloaf, Prince, Anastasia etc.

Born late '58, when his father was 67 and his mother 45, who
claimed he was a virgin birth – she was prone to exaggeration!
Peter nearly died from an anaphylactic shock when he was 25
whilst working in India, which made him appreciate life. It's
only Rock'n'Roll, but Peter thinks you will like it...

Peter Cook   www.academy-of-rock.co.uk

Acknowledgements

I am grateful to the following people, without which this book would not have come to life:

Peter Birkett, who designed the visual concept for this book. Peter runs Das Ist Design e-mail dasistdesign@talk21.com

Rowena Sian Morgan, for her willingness to model for the cover photos in the middle of winter. Rowena is in charge of Business Development for BASCA – The British Academy of Songwriters, Composers and Authors www.basca.org.uk/

Piers Taylor Photography for cover shots, pictures of Rowena Sian Morgan and various other pictures. Find him on Facebook and by phone at 07906 533604

Richard Strange, enigmatic musician, actor, writer and bon viveur. The Godfather of Punk according to Johnny Rotten www.richardstrange.com

Bill Nelson, a continuous source of creativity across my lifetime: musician, artist, writer, long-distance dreamer www.billnelson.com

Lindsay Wakelin for her punk rock photographs www.lindsaywakelinphotography.com

Jason Dodds for his photographs of rock professors www.jasondoddphotography.com

Bernie Tormé, guitar supremo, rock god and occasional musical sparring partner www.barnroom.co.uk

Dr Andrew Sentance CBE, Senior Economic Adviser to PricewaterhouseCoopers and the product of a genetic fusion of John Maynard Keynes, Robert Plant and Peter Gabriel www.sentance.com

John Howitt, musical collaborator, session musician and a rock amidst Rock'n'Roll chaos.

Steve Mostyn, Associate Fellow, Saïd Business School, Executive Education. Steve may be reached at www.steve-mostyn.com

Christophe Godin, guitar maestro, humorist and teacher www.christophegodin.com

Scott McGill, for fearless exploration of the art and discipline of improvisation www.scottmcgill.com

Richard Laermer, for sheer audacity, great humour and wonderful ideas www.laermer.com

Martin Bostock for the photograph of Bill Nelson and Orchestra Futura www.martinbostock.co.uk

Andy Wooler for his excellent contributions to the article on opera. www.andywooler.info/wordpress Twitter @awooler

Michael Michalko for his superb article on creativity. www.creativethinking.net

Daevid Allen for kindly sharing the cover of his stunning album "Camembert Electrique" by French psychedelic jazz rockers Gong, made all the more poignant by the recent news of a terminal cancer condition. Thanks to Dave Sturt for making this happen www.planetgong.co.uk

Christof Zürn at Music Thinking for his contribution to the article on climate via the example of Richard Wagner www.musicthinking.com

Lee Phillips of ME1 TV for including me in his team of people as an interviewer of music giants from George Clinton to Roberta Flack and beyond www.me1.tv

Peter Cook   www.academy-of-rock.co.uk

Christina Jansen – Photographer extraordinaire, who has photographed everyone from Muhammed Ali to Robert Plant, Emma Thompson and beyond www.cjansenphotography.com

Patti Russo, who trusted me to help her develop the next phase of her career based on an initial meeting over a cigarette www.patti-rocks.com

Lois Acton who arranged interviews with George Clinton, the Godfather of Funk, Nile Rodgers and Sheila E

Tom Peters, the grand daddy of business leadership and a great inspiration www.tompeters.com

Ben Weinlick – Creative Collaborator at The Think Jar Collective www.thinkjarcollective.com

David D'Souza at the CIPD for his article on the Bruno Mars HR disciplinary interview. Find him on Twitter at @dds180

Bibliography

Argyris, C., and Schön, D., (1974). *Organizational Learning: A Theory of Action Perspective*, Reading, MA: Addison-Wesley

Branson, Richard., (2014). *The Virgin Way*, London: Portfolio

Cook, Peter, (1998). *Best Practice Creativity*, Aldershot: Gower.

Cook, Peter, (2006). *Sex, Leadership and Rock'n'Roll: Leadership Lessons from the Academy of Rock*, Carmarthen: Crown House.

Cook, Peter, (2011). *Punk Rock People Management*, Teynham: Cultured Llama.

Csikszentmihalyi, M., (1990). *Flow: The Psychology of Optimal Experience*, New York: Harper and Row.

de Bono, Edward (1984). *Lateral Thinking for Management*, London: Penguin.

Ericsson, K. Anders, (2009). *Development of Professional Expertise: Toward Measurement of Expert Performance and Design of Optimal Learning Environments*, New York: Cambridge University Press.

Festinger, Leon, (1957). *A Theory of Cognitive Dissonance*, London: Pinter and Martin.

Furnham, Adrian, (2009). *50 Psychology Ideas You Really Need To Know*, London: Quercus.

Furnham, Adrian, (2010). *The Elephant In the Boardroom: The Causes of Leadership Derailment*, London: Palgrave Macmillan.

Ghiselin, Brewster (1985). *The Creative Process*, Berkeley: University of California Press.

Gladwell, Malcolm, (2009). *Outliers: The Story of Success*, London: Penguin.

Gleick, James, (1987). *Chaos*, London: Abacus.

Godin, Seth, (2008). *Tribes: We need you to lead us*, London, Penguin.

Hammer, M., and Champy, J., (1991). *Reengineering the Corporation: A manifesto for business revolution*, New York: Harper Collins.

Handy, Charles, (1989). *The Age of Unreason*, London: Arrow Books.

Handy, Charles, (1994). *The Empty Raincoat*, London: Random House.

Henry, Jane and Walker, David, (1991). *Managing Innovation*, London: Sage.

Henry, Jane, (1991). *Creative Management*, London: Sage.

Johnson, G., (1987). *Strategic Change and the Management Process*, Oxford: Blackwell.

Isenberg, S.G., and Treffinger, D.J., (1985). *Creative Problem Solving, The Basic Course*, Buffalo: Bearly.

Kao, John, (1996). *Jamming: The Art and Discipline of Business Creativity*, New York: Harper Business.

Kirton, Michael, (1989). *Adaptors and Innovators*, London: Routledge.

Koestler, Arthur, (1964). *The Act of Creation*, London: Hutchinson.

Krause, Donald G., (1995). *The Art of War for Executives*, London: Nicholas Brealey Publishing.

Laermer, Richard, (2007). *Punk Marketing: Get Off Your Ass and Join the Revolution*, New York: Harper Business.

Levtin, Daniel., (2014). *The Organised Mind, Thinking Straight in the Age of Information Overload*, London: Random House.

McKean, Michael, (2000). *This is Spinal Tap: The Official Com-*

panion, London: Bloombsbury.

Miller, Arthur I., (2000). *Insights of Genius*, Cambridge Mass: The MIT Press.

Mintzberg, Henry, (1989). *Mintzberg on Management*, New York: The Free Press.

Morgan, Gareth, (1993). *Imagination: The Art of Creative Management*, London: Sage.

Nelson, Bill, (2004). *Diary of a Hyperdreamer*, Hebden Bridge: Pomona.

Nelson, Bill, (2010). *Painted From Memory (Sketches for an Autobiography)*, Wakefield: Autumn Ink Industries.

Peters, Tom, (2010). *The Little Big Things: 163 Ways to Pursue Excellence at Work*, New York: Harper Business.

Peters, Tom (1989). *Thriving on Chaos: Handbook for a Management Revolution*, New York: Harper Business.

Peters, Tom, (2004). *In Search of Excellence: Lessons from America's Best-Run Companies*, London: Profile Books.

Pink, Daniel, (2008). *A Whole New Mind: Why Right-Brainers Will Rule the Future*, New York: Marshall Cavendish.

Senge, Peter, (1990). *The Fifth Discipline*, London: Random Century.

Sloane, Paul, (2011). *A Guide to Open Innovation and Crowdsourcing: Advice from Leading Experts in the Field*, London: Kogan Page.

Sutton-Reeves, Paul, (2008). *Music in Dreamland – Bill Nelson and Be-Bop Deluxe*, London: Helter Skelter Publishing.

Strange, Richard, (2002). *Punks and Drunks and Flicks and Kicks*, London: Andre Deutsch.

Wallas, G., (1926), *The Art of Thought*, New York: Franklin Watts.

Index

O

Oasis 40, 184
Observability 199
OK Computer 41
Opera vii, 27, 29, 33, 34
organisation design 142, 283
organisation development 287
Osmonds, The 136
Ozzy Osbourne 49, 50, 75, 142, 156, 288

P

Patti Smith 186
Paula Yates 28
Paul McKenna 243
Paul Weller 40, 184
Pepsi 138
performance appraisals 159
performance related pay 160
persistence 188, 193
personal mastery ix, 71, 73, 263
Peter Grant 2, 18, 21
Peter Senge 71, 214, 273
Pfizer iii, 93, 94, 146, 234, 286
physics 40, 82
Placebo 274
playfulness 207
Post-it Note 110, 188, 193
Practice 70, 71, 94, 126, 132, 153, 292
preparation 70, 150, 154
PricewaterhouseCoopers 4, 54, 290
Prince viii, 7, 10, 24, 40, 50, 70, 107, 111, 120, 142, 149, 150, 151, 152, 153, 154, 238, 264, 283, 288
Procter and Gamble 45
Procter & Gamble 45, 137

project management 24, 25
psychedelia 77
Psychedelic Furs, The 186
psychological environment 157, 159, 187, 189, 283
psychology 219
punk 26, 29, 61, 85, 130, 131, 132, 136, 137, 143, 176, 240, 247, 282, 283, 287, 289
Punk Marketing viii, 135, 138, 293
Punk Rock 61, 133, 134, 135, 292
Punk Rock People Management 61, 135, 292

Q

Queen iii, 34, 40, 119, 145, 258, 287, 288

R

Ramones, The 176
random stimuli 180
Ravel 126
Red Noise 111, 263
reinvention ix, 3, 41, 168, 211, 212, 243, 252, 258, 263, 264, 265, 268, 269, 271, 284
Relative advantage 199
REM 284
Rembrant 110
responsiveness 2, 281
reversal 180
reward 45, 119, 221, 232
Richard Bandler 204, 243
Richard Branson 3, 78, 83, 142, 181, 193, 195, 196, 249, 283, 286
Richard Jobson 181
Richard Laermer viii, 61, 85, 135, 139, 282, 290

Peter Cook   www.academy-of-rock.co.uk

Catch us Live

If you like this book you will love us live, so book one of our outstanding events or full leadership development programmes, mixing world-class business ideas with music.

Conferences and events – Some examples:

- Riffs and myths of leadership
- What's new pussycat? – Innovation excellence
- Blowin' away the blues – Motivation master class
- Jazz, jamming and corporate improvisation
- Fifty shades of business excellence

WEB www.academy-of-rock.co.uk

Business, Organisation Development and Coaching

Designed to your specific needs and expectations:
www.humdyn.co.uk

Check our Music – Business Blog for regular updates:
www.humandynamics.wordpress.com

www.academy-of-rock.co.uk   Peter Cook

Cultured Llama Publishing
Poems | Stories | Curious Things

Cultured Llama was born in a converted stable. This creature of humble birth drank greedily from the creative source of the poets, writers, artists and musicians that visited, and soon the llama fulfilled the destiny of its given name.

Cultured Llama is a publishing house, a multi-arts events promoter and a fundraiser for charity. It aspires to quality from the first creative thought through to the finished product.

www.culturedllama.co.uk

Other non-fiction published by Cultured Llama

Do It Yourself: A History of Music in Medway by Stephen H. Morris. Paperback; 504pp; 229×152mm; 978-0-9926485-2-7; March 2015

The definitive and indispensable guide to Medway music. Mixing oral history with profiles of the best singles, EPs and albums to come out of the Medway Towns since the mid-1970s, Morris tells the story of how performers such as Billy Childish, The Dentists and Lupen Crook have produced music whose influence extends far beyond the reach of five small towns in the north of Kent.

**Punk Rock People Management:
A No-Nonsense Guide to Hiring, Inspiring and Firing Staff**
by Peter Cook. Paperback; 38pp;
229×152mm; 978-0-9932119-0-4;
March 2015

Punk Rock People Management
strips down HR to the bare
essentials for busy people and
those who are sick of HR jargon
getting in the way of running a
business. In the spirit of punk,
each chapter is just one page
long, which means that you can
read a chapter in less time than
it takes to pogo to a Sex Pistols or Linkin Park song! *Punk
Rock People Management* is organised using the classic Life,
Sex and Death HR cycle, in other words Hiring, Inspiring and
Firing. If you have to get things done with people and can't
get no satisfaction from an HR textbook, try *Punk Rock People
Management* for a refreshing difference.

Lightning Source UK Ltd.
Milton Keynes UK
UKOW02f0133160515

251659UK00001B/9/P